THE PROCRASTINATION SOLUTION

DAILY STRATEGIES TO TAKE IMMEDIATE ACTION TO OVERCOME SELF-IMPOSED DELAYS, BUILD CONSISTENT MOMENTUM, AND CREATE UNSTOPPABLE PRODUCTIVITY

BOBBY L. BUTLER

Bridge Publishers, LLC

Bridge Publishers, LLC | Lebanon, TN

Publisher's Note: The information in this book is based on the author's experience and research. While the author and publisher have made every effort to provide accurate and up-to-date information, they assume no responsibility for errors, omissions, or contrary interpretation of the subject matter herein.

Library of Congress Control Number: 2025922891
ISBN-13 (Paperback): 979-8-9932981-0-8
ISBN-13 (Hardcover): 979-8-9932981-1-5
ISBN-13 (eBook): 979-8-9932981-2-2

First Edition
Printed in the United States of America
10 9 8 7 6 5 4 3 2 1

Edited by Editor World LLC
Interior designed by Ultimate Book Formatting
Cover designed by 100Covers

CONTENTS

INTRODUCTION

Let's get real for a moment. You know that feeling when your to-do list is growing by the second, but you can't make yourself move? You sit at your desk, staring at the same email or spreadsheet, and suddenly an hour disappears. Maybe you scroll through your phone. Perhaps you convince yourself you'll start after just one more cup of coffee. And then, somehow, the day slips away and the thing you swore you'd finish still isn't done. If you've ever felt stuck in that loop, you've found the right book.

I get it because I've lived it. For years, I was the King of "I'll do it tomorrow." I'd make grand plans and break them by noon. My desk was a graveyard of half-finished projects and sticky notes of things I meant to start. I'd binge-watch productivity hacks but rarely act on any of them. It wasn't laziness. It wasn't a lack of ambition. It was something deeper—a silent force that kept me frozen even when I wanted to move. And honestly, it made me feel frustrated and ashamed.

But something changed. After missing a big deadline—one that really mattered—I hit a wall. I couldn't hide from the truth anymore. I had to admit that procrastination wasn't just a bad habit; it was controlling my life. That was the first step. The next step was figuring out why and how to break free. It wasn't easy, and it certainly wasn't quick. But it was possible. And that journey is what brought me here, writing this book for you.

Procrastination is everywhere. It's the silent epidemic nobody wants to talk about. We joke about it, but underneath, it's a painful reality. It eats away at our confidence. It keeps us from getting that promotion, finishing that side project, or just having a peaceful evening without guilt. For those of you juggling work and home responsibilities, it can feel like you're failing on all fronts. For anyone hustling to make their mark, it can feel like you're falling behind for no good reason. The pain is real, and it's personal.

Maybe you've tried to fix it before. You bought planners, downloaded apps, and made promises to yourself. Or, you got inspired by a YouTube video, only to find yourself back at square one a week later. If you're skeptical, I don't blame you. Procrastination is sneaky. It makes big promises and delivers only regret. You might wonder if there's a way out. I'm here to tell you there is.

This book isn't about shaming you or presenting you with yet another impossible system to follow. It's about providing you with real, daily strategies that you can actually use. No fluff. No magical thinking. Just simple, proven ways to take action right now, even when you don't feel like it. The promise of this book is simple: you will learn how to overcome self-imposed delays, build momentum, and make productivity automatic. Not because you changed who you are, but because you finally understand how to work with your own brain—not against it.

What makes this book different? For starters, I won't ask you to wake up at 5 a.m. or completely overhaul your personality. I know you're busy. I know your life is already full. Instead, you'll get bite-sized strategies that fit into your real daily life—whether you're racing between meetings or squeezing in work after the kids go to bed. I'll show you how tiny shifts, done daily, add up to unstoppable momentum.

The structure of this book is simple and flexible, designed for you to take what you need when you need it. Think of it like a *choose-your-*

own-adventure for getting stuff done. You can jump straight to the parts that speak to you or read straight through for an overall reset. If you're overwhelmed, start small. If you're ready to go big, there's a path for that too.

Pause right here and think about one thing you've been putting off. It could be small or huge. Picture it clearly. How long has it been haunting you? How would your life change if you finally tackled it? Hold onto that thought as you move through these pages. This isn't just a book—it's a toolbox. Grab what works; skip what doesn't.

One last thing—and it's important: **you are not lazy or broken.**

Procrastination is not a character flaw; it's a pattern of behavior that can be changed—one small step at a time. I'm going to walk with you through every chapter, sharing what worked (and what flopped) for me. I'll offer support, honesty, and a few laughs along the way.

So, are you ready? Ready to stop letting procrastination decide your future? Ready to discover how much you can actually get done without losing your mind or your joy? Your journey starts now. Open to any page. Try one idea. See what happens. The actions you take could change everything. Let's do this together.

CHAPTER 1

WHY YOU PROCRASTINATE —AND WHY IT'S NOT YOUR FAULT

You know that weird sense of relief you feel when you avoid a tough task, even if it means dealing with more stress later? I know that feeling all too well. I'll never forget the morning I spent staring at an urgent work email instead of answering it. It wasn't even a complicated message. I just felt this heavy dread in my chest, like any reply I could craft would be wrong. So, I kept switching tabs, checking the weather, and reading headlines that didn't interest me. By the time lunch rolled around, my anxiety had doubled, and the email was still haunting me.

If this sounds familiar, you're not alone. Most people blame themselves for moments like these. However, there's something deeper happening —a silent battle inside your mind that shapes your choices, even when you desperately want to act.

THE HIDDEN SCIENCE OF SELF-DELAY

Procrastination isn't just a quirky habit or poor time management; it's a biological reaction—a full-body experience driven by ancient wiring in your brain.

Let's break it down: two powerful forces are constantly pulling you in opposite directions. One is the limbic system, the part of your brain that handles emotions, urges, and survival instincts. It's lightning-fast and always on the lookout for comfort or danger. The other is the prefrontal cortex, the "thinker" that handles planning, logic, and self-control. When you want to focus on a long-term goal, like preparing for a presentation or writing that overdue report, your prefrontal cortex takes the wheel. But when discomfort, anxiety, or uncertainty hit, your limbic system slams on the brakes and yanks you toward the nearest escape—scrolling, snacking, or anything but the hard thing in front of you.

Here's where things get tricky. Your brain is wired to reward you for short-term comfort. When you dodge an uncomfortable task in favor of scrolling through Instagram or making another coffee run, your limbic system releases dopamine. This feel-good chemical reinforces the behavior, essentially training your brain to associate avoidance with a sense of reward. This creates what psychologists call *present bias*, your mind's tendency to value immediate pleasure or relief over future benefits. Even if you know finishing that project will make your life better next week, the relief of not dealing with it right now feels far more tempting. This isn't a personal failure; it's a universal quirk of how the brain operates (Lieberman, 2019). fMRI scans show that when faced with a choice between now and later, the emotional part of your brain shouts out first. The logical planner has to fight hard just to be heard.

Researchers like Tim Pychyl have found that procrastination has less to do with laziness or a lack of discipline and far more to do with how we manage emotions in the moment (Shatz, n.d.). When a task triggers fear, self-doubt, or boredom, your brain tries to protect you by steering you away from that discomfort. Joseph Ferrari's studies delve even deeper, revealing that roughly one in five adults is a chronic procrastinators who struggle with these patterns daily (Ferrari, 2020). So, procrastination isn't rare; it's shockingly common.

Stress and anxiety can turbocharge procrastination cycles. The moment you see a daunting project pop up on your to-do list, your body reacts as if it's facing a wild animal rather than a spreadsheet or an email: your heart rate climbs, your shoulders tense, and your palms sweat.

Your body is signaling "danger," even though you're just staring at a screen. In these moments, the limbic system takes over, urging you to retreat into safety by cleaning your desk for the third time or re-reading old Slack threads.

Let me share two real-life stories that illustrate how this plays out in everyday life. Sarah is a sharp marketing manager who crushes her weekly tasks—until presentation day arrives. The night before, she freezes at her laptop, cycling through slides but never finalizing them. Her mind races with what-ifs: what if I forget my lines? What if they hate my ideas? Instead of rehearsing or asking for feedback, she distracts herself with busy work and barely sleeps. The next morning, she rushes out the door, feeling unprepared and ashamed.

Then there's Alex, a talented software engineer who loves solving problems—except when it comes to bug reports. When he sees a new ticket flagged as "urgent," his stomach knots, and he pushes it aside to work on easier tasks or tweak old code he already understands. The ticket stays open until the deadline is hours away, and stress finally forces him to act. Alex knows this cycle hurts his confidence and reputation at work, but each time it plays out the same way.

These stories aren't about laziness or a lack of intelligence; they're about brains that become stuck in survival mode when faced with challenges or uncertainty. Procrastination is your mind's attempt to dodge discomfort—even if it means doubling your stress later. Science shows this is not your fault; it's how human beings naturally respond to challenging emotions and overwhelming pressure (Insights Psychology, 2024).

If you recognize yourself in Sarah's, Alex's, or any of my opening stories, take a breath and let yourself off the hook for a moment. You're not broken; you're human. The urge to avoid pain is hardwired and powerful, but understanding the science behind it gives you the power to make new choices from now on.

PROCRASTINATION IS NOT LAZINESS—IT'S A HABIT LOOP

If you've ever flopped on your couch after a marathon day at work, grabbed the remote, and disappeared into the world of Netflix, you understand what it means to seek escape. But here's the thing: that urge to escape doesn't mean you're lazy. Most people who struggle with procrastination are far from apathetic. You care—sometimes too much. You want to do well, to finish what you start, to prove yourself at work and home. The problem isn't a lack of ambition. It's the loop you fall into when stress and discomfort drown out everything else. Laziness means you don't care about the effort or outcome. Procrastinators care so profoundly that the fear of falling short makes them retreat, even as their minds race with everything left undone.

Consider this familiar scenario: you sit down at your desk, knowing you need to draft a tough report. Even before your fingers touch the keyboard, a wave of anxiety hits. Maybe it's the pressure to impress your manager or the uncertainty about where to begin. That anxiety is the "trigger." Your body tenses, and your mind scrambles for an escape route. Almost on autopilot, you click over to your favorite social media app or open another tab to check the news "for just five minutes." That's the "routine." For a moment, you feel lighter. The stress fades into the background; cat videos or trending headlines take over. This is the "reward": temporary relief, a fleeting sense of comfort that soothes your nerves for now.

Each time you repeat this cycle, your brain learns. It connects avoidance with emotional payoff. The more you run this loop, the more ingrained it becomes (Wood et al., 2023). You're not seeking laziness; you're seeking relief. The loop gets stronger not because you want to do less but because your mind has learned that dodging unpleasant tasks brings short-term pleasure or peace. That's why even high achievers—people who routinely crush big projects or juggle multiple roles—can find themselves stuck. Procrastination is an emotional coping strategy that masquerades as "just taking a break." Over time, it becomes a habit that feels impossible to break.

Let me walk you through an episode that will sound familiar to many professionals. Picture a junior lawyer, fresh out of law school and eager to prove herself in a competitive firm. She's been assigned a legal brief —her first big solo project. She sits down in her cubicle late one afternoon, determined to crush it, but the blank document feels like a mountain staring back at her. The trigger: fear of judgment from senior partners and worry that any mistake will haunt her reputation. Her mind races through worst-case scenarios—typos, missed precedents, angry emails from her boss—her stomach knots, and her palms sweat.

Instead of typing the opening line, she tells herself a quick scroll through LinkedIn will help her "clear her head." Perhaps she'll find inspiration or discover what her peers are doing. She stares at updates from old classmates and news from other firms, becoming both distracted and disconnected from her work. This routine stretches on for half an hour before she even realizes what she's doing. The reward: her anxiety about the brief fades into the background for just a little while. She's not lazy—she's overwhelmed—and wants to escape the discomfort of getting started.

This cycle repeats for days until the deadline looms too close to ignore. Then comes the late-night scramble as adrenaline kicks in, and she finally throws herself into the work—not because she found new motivation, but because panic replaces dread as the trigger. And, after turning in the brief, she berates herself for waiting so long, convinced she'll never break the cycle.

But here's what matters: every step in that episode follows the habit loop—trigger (anxiety), routine (avoidance), and reward (relief). The loop is efficient, providing fast feedback (Wood et al., 2015). Your brain latches onto this pattern because it works in the short term, even if it sabotages you later.

If you've beaten yourself up over this pattern, pause and notice the difference between not caring and caring so much that it paralyzes you. Procrastinators are often some of the most diligent people around; their avoidance is rooted not in laziness but in deep investment and fear of letting themselves—or others—down.

To break this habit loop, start by mapping out your own procrastination cycle. Next time you notice yourself putting something off, jot down what sparked the avoidance (the trigger), what behavior you slipped into (the routine), and what feeling followed (the reward). You'll start to see patterns emerge, not just in what you do but in how you seek comfort when tasks threaten your sense of competence or control.

When you recognize this loop in your own life—not just once, but as a recurring theme—it becomes easier to disrupt it. You can't fight what you can't see. Awareness is your first foothold out of the rut. If you've spent years thinking, "I'm just lazy," try swapping that old script for "I'm stuck in a habit loop my brain wants to repeat." That shift alone can soften self-blame and create space for genuine change.

YOUR UNIQUE PROCRASTINATION PROFILE (WITH DIAGNOSTIC QUIZ)

It's easy to think procrastination feels the same for everyone, but that's just not true. The way you put things off, the things you avoid, and how you try to cope all shape your personal "procrastination style." This is where real change begins: understanding what's actually behind your delays rather than trying to force yourself into a fix that never quite fits you in the first place.

One-size-fits-all fixes fall apart because what works for a deadline junkie won't help someone paralyzed by too many choices. If you've ever wondered why "just do it" never worked for you or why you keep repeating the same behaviors, no matter how many times you swear this week will be different, it's because you haven't zeroed in on your own pattern yet. Once you do, you can target the real issue, not just the symptoms.

There are four main archetypes that recur frequently in research and real life: the Perfectionist, the Overwhelmed Avoider, the Thrill-Seeker, and the Decision Paralysis type. Each has its own flavor, triggers, and quirks, and knowing which one sounds most like you can make all the difference.

The Perfectionist is the classic over-editor, never satisfied with anything that is less than flawless. If you find yourself rewriting emails late into the night, triple-checking every word, or hesitating to send a Slack message because it doesn't sound "just right," you're likely in this camp. It's not that you don't care—it's that you care so much it's nearly impossible to let go. At home, perfectionists might stall on organizing a closet because they can't decide on the perfect system, or they spend hours debating what to write in a birthday card until it's easier not to send one at all. At work, they'll invest too much time tinkering with PowerPoint slides and miss out on feedback that could have been gained by sharing a draft sooner.

Next comes the Overwhelmed Avoider. Large or unclear projects are their kryptonite. If you've ever looked at a new assignment, felt your chest tighten, and then immediately decided to "deal with it later," this may be your type. You might ignore quarterly reports until your manager reminds you three times. At home, you may put off tax preparation until April 15 or leave laundry in piled baskets because starting feels like scaling a mountain. The common thread is avoidance, not due to laziness, but because the task feels so massive or vague that any action seems pointless or exhausting.

The Thrill-Seeker feeds off deadlines and being in crisis mode. They need the rush of racing the clock to feel alive and productive. If you finish projects at 2:00 a.m., tell yourself, "I work best under pressure," or get that strange satisfaction from pulling off last-minute miracles, this will likely describe you. Maybe you leave travel packing until the morning of your flight or don't begin writing until the night before a proposal is due. In office settings, thrill-seekers might wait until meeting reminders appear before preparing their slides, relying on adrenaline to get them through.

Then there's Decision Paralysis type—the chronic second-guesser. Too many options freeze them solid. If you've ever spent an entire lunch hour toggling between two project management tools and ending up picking neither or scrolling through endless task apps without choosing one, this may be your world. At home, deciding what to cook or which gym class to join becomes a week-long ordeal. These folks often research every option to death, waiting for a sense of certainty that never arrives. The cost is momentum: action stalls out because no choice feels quite right.

Understanding which style dominates your life gives you clarity—not a label or a limit. Maybe you see pieces of yourself in more than one archetype—many people do. You might be a Perfectionist when writing reports, but a Thrill-Seeker when cleaning your apartment. The point is to identify your strongest patterns so you can start working with them rather than letting them run wild in the background.

Why does this matter so much? Because advice that works wonders for one profile can backfire for someone else. A Perfectionist might need to practice sending imperfect drafts and celebrating progress over polish. In contrast, an Overwhelmed Avoider needs to break big tasks into micro-steps with visible wins at each stage. The Thrill-Seeker can build mini-deadlines into their day to avoid all-or-nothing panic cycles, while Decision Paralysis types get relief from setting time limits on choices or trusting small bets over perfect plans.

QUIZ: What's Your Procrastination Profile?

Instructions: Read each statement and check all that feel true for you most of the time. Then, follow the scoring guide below.

- ☐ A. I often revise and overthink emails, documents, or plans before sharing them.
- ☐ B. Big or unclear tasks make me freeze and avoid starting until I'm forced.
- ☐ C. I usually wait until just before a deadline to get started because I need pressure to focus.
- ☐ D. I delay decisions by endlessly comparing options or researching instead of choosing.

Your Results:

- If A: You're likely a Perfectionist
- If B: You're likely an Overwhelmed Avoider
- If C: You're likely a Thrill-Seeker

- If D: You're likely a Decision Paralysis type

If you checked multiple boxes, circle your top two, then ask yourself: "Which of these two patterns causes me the most trouble or happens most often?" That's your primary type; focus your solutions there first, but keep strategies for your secondary type in reserve.

Armed with this insight, keep your profile in mind as you move forward. Your procrastination isn't random—it follows a script that can be rewritten once you know what role you're playing.

Want to dig deeper? If you're curious about your specific triggers and how your procrastination patterns show up in different situations, check out the comprehensive procrastination profile assessment tool located on our resource hub. This expanded quiz will help you better understand what derails you and provide strategies to address your unique patterns.

Use the link here: https://bit.ly/MyProfileAssessment

Or use this QR code:

THE ROLE OF PERFECTIONISM, FEAR, AND OVERWHELM

Perfectionism is a sneaky villain disguised as ambition. You might take pride in high standards. You may be the one who always spots the typos, who finds the missing piece in a proposal, who double-checks every detail before sending anything out the door. However, for many high-achieving women and men, this drive for excellence can quietly mutate into a roadblock. Instead of launching forward, you freeze at the start line, convinced that if it isn't flawless, it's safer not to begin at all.

I recall a colleague who was brilliant at her job—a woman everyone regarded as the "go-to" expert for new ideas. Yet, she spent hours rewriting her pitch decks, second-guessing her phrasing, and tweaking her slides until the deadline left her no choice but to go ahead and submit. Instead of feeling accomplished, she'd apologize for imperfections no one else noticed. Her story is not rare. Research shows perfectionism rarely leads to higher achievement. It leads to hesitation, missed opportunities, and burnout (Boyes, 2020). The "if I can't do it perfectly, I won't start at all" mindset traps you in a cycle—you wait for the perfect plan and the perfect moment, but neither ever arrives.

Fear operates in the background like an invisible puppeteer, pulling your strings in subtle ways. Sometimes, it's fear of failure—worry that you'll crash in front of everyone if you try something new or bold. At other times, it's the fear of negative feedback—the sting of someone saying your work isn't good enough or questioning your ideas. There's also a quieter kind of fear: fear of success. What if you nail this project? What if more will be expected next time? As the stakes get higher, the pressure grows.

Take the case of a product manager in a fast-moving tech company. He has an idea that could streamline his team's workflow. He spends days fleshing out every angle, overpreparing for objections, but when the weekly meeting comes, he hesitates. His heart races. He asks himself, "What if they hate it? What if I sound foolish?" Instead of speaking up, he stays silent and later feels frustrated for not contributing. This fear doesn't come from a lack of confidence or skill; it comes from an urge to avoid pain—whether it's embarrassment, rejection, or even unexpected responsibility.

Overwhelm is another beast entirely. Some days, it feels like you're drowning under a tidal wave of tasks—Slack messages pinging, emails piling up, calendars double-booked. When the demands stack up and goals blur together, your brain seems to shut down as a survival tactic.

You sit at your desk, staring at the screen as your mind bounces from one urgent task to the next. At home, you might have a list that runs onto a second page: groceries, birthday gifts, laundry, and doctor appointments. When everything feels equally important and nothing is clear, starting anything seems impossible. Ambiguity—unclear instructions, shifting expectations—makes this worse. If your manager sends you a vague request or your client keeps changing their mind about the project scope, you might freeze up—not because you don't care—but from lack of clarity.

Most people carry a blend of these emotional drivers: perfectionism in one area, fear in another, overwhelm everywhere else. These are powerful forces shaping your choices before you even realize it. They don't announce themselves with blinking lights or sirens; they creep in as hesitation, nervousness, or a sudden urge to do something—anything—other than what matters most.

Visualization Exercise: Pinpoint Your Emotional Driver

Close your eyes for a moment and remember the last task you put off —big or small. Maybe it was sending feedback to your team, booking an appointment you've been dreading, or starting that overdue report. Replay the scene in your mind. Where were you sitting? What did your workspace look like? Who else was around? Now ask yourself: what feeling bubbled up first as you faced it? Was it the heavy pressure of wanting everything perfect? Was it the tightness in your chest that comes with fear of failing or being judged? Did you feel lost in a sea of tasks with no clue where to begin? Notice which emotion stands out most strongly.

Grab your phone or a notebook and jot down your answer. Don't over-think it; just write the emotion or thought that hit first: "I wanted it perfect," "I was afraid of looking stupid," "I felt totally swamped." This is your starting point. Knowing whether perfectionism, fear, or over-whelm drives your avoidance is the first step to choosing strategies that work for you—not just generic advice that ignores what's real for you right now.

DEBUNKING "WILLPOWER" AND OTHER PRODUCTIVITY MYTHS

For years, I bought into the idea that if I just tried a little harder, forced myself to grind through distractions, or "wanted it badly enough," I'd finally get a handle on procrastination. This belief is everywhere. Whole industries are built on selling *grit* and *hustle* as the cures for every problem. Podcasts, Instagram feeds, and even well-meaning friends repeat the same advice: dig deeper, summon more willpower, and outwork the urge to put things off. It sounds reasonable—at least until you're exhausted, staring at the same unfinished task and wondering why sheer determination isn't cutting it.

The truth is that willpower isn't an endless well you can draw from whenever you need it. Roy Baumeister's research revolutionized the world of productivity by demonstrating that willpower operates much like a muscle, becoming fatigued with use (Boogaard, 2023). Every decision you make during the day—what to wear, what to eat, how to reply to that tricky email—chips away at your reserves. By the time you face your most important work, you may find yourself running on fumes. This is called "ego depletion." It explains why even the most disciplined people can crumble after a long day of choices and stress.

Decision fatigue is everywhere in modern life. If you've ever found yourself unable to pick what to have for dinner after a day packed with meetings and micro-decisions, you've felt its effects. Each choice drains your mental energy until even small tasks feel overwhelming. The more hats you wear—project manager, parent, friend, partner— the quicker your willpower gets used up. When people tell you to "just push through," they're ignoring the reality that pushing gets harder the more you have on your plate.

Platitudes like "work harder" or "motivation is all you need" can do real harm. They sound motivating at first but turn toxic when they don't match the chaos of your day-to-day life. Hustle culture glorifies sleep deprivation and relentless effort. The result? Burnout, resentment, and a constant sense of falling short, especially when you see others on social media "crushing it" while you're just trying to stay afloat. If grit alone worked, high achievers would never hit walls.

Instead, many burn out and end up procrastinating more as their energy tanks.

I've lived through those cycles myself, fueling up on coffee and pep talks only to crash and wonder what went wrong. The more I tried to power through with force of will, the less progress I made. I'd set ambitious goals, white-knuckle my way for a few days, and then collapse into avoidance when my energy ran out. The guilt would double down making it even harder to try again. Sound familiar?

It's easy to believe that people who get things done have superhuman discipline or some secret source of motivation. But the real difference isn't in raw willpower—it's in the systems and environments they build around themselves. Research shows that small tweaks to your routine or workspace—such as preparing your desk before logging off or turning off phone notifications during deep work—make demanding tasks less intimidating and reduce the friction of getting started (Scroggs, 2024). Consistency comes from habits and cues, not from waking up every day ready to fight the same battle with yourself.

Self-compassion matters even more than discipline over the long haul. When you beat yourself up for slipping, your brain associates work with pain and shame, making avoidance even sweeter next time. However, when you view setbacks as a normal part of life—something every human experiences—you create space to try again without fear or self-loathing (Neff, n.d.). This shift isn't just softer; it's smarter. People who show kindness to themselves after a failure are more likely to bounce back and keep moving forward. (Self-compassion is covered in detail in Chapter 8.)

In the coming chapters, I'll share practical ways to make your environment work for you rather than against you. You'll learn how to design systems that do the heavy lifting so your willpower can take a break. We'll talk about routines that stick even during wild weeks, tiny habits that build momentum, and how to recover from setbacks without getting stuck in shame spirals. My goal isn't to turn you into a productivity machine—it's to help you build a life where taking action feels natural, even when motivation is scarce.

For now, give yourself permission to let go of the myth that more brute force is what you need. You're not weak when willpower runs out— you're normal. Real change comes from building reliable, actionable support around your goals and treating yourself with patience rather than criticism. If you start replacing self-blame with better systems and a little compassion, momentum follows in ways grit alone never will.

CHAPTER 2
MEET YOUR TRIGGERS —IDENTIFYING YOUR REAL OBSTACLES

THE ANATOMY OF AN OVERWHELMING TO-DO LIST

Imagine opening your favorite task app or planner, ready to list every project, errand, or idea swirling in your head. Five tasks turn into ten: "Finish quarterly analysis," "Fix the slide deck," "Plan team offsite." As the list grows, the initial sense of control fades, replaced by anxiety and paralysis. Instead of working, you find yourself scrolling social media, grabbing more coffee, or rewriting the list again. For many, this isn't just frustrating—it's immobilizing. Why do lists provoke such dread?

The issue isn't just the length of your list, but the vagueness and size of each task. Broad items like "Work on report" or "Handle marketing stuff" leave your brain unsure where to start, making each job feel insurmountable. Without clear next steps, your mind registers every task as a mountain, not a series of manageable hills.

Tasks like "update website" or "organize files" don't clarify what completion looks like, so you defer them indefinitely. This ambiguity leads to avoidance in disguise—choosing busywork, endlessly tweaking the list, or switching between productivity apps rather than taking real action. The more tasks blur together without deadlines or priorities, the heavier the burden feels.

Ambiguous tasks force your mind to decide anew what to do each time you see them. If the "planned project" sits untouched, it's a daily reminder that you don't know where to begin—these open loops drain your focus little by little (Boogaard, 2023). You may procrastinate on even writing your list, knowing it will leave you drained.

Overwhelm also shows in smaller ways: endless tab-switching, boredom snacking, or plain mental fatigue from merely facing the list. You might take on easy new requests to avoid larger, looming tasks or duplicate simple items just to enjoy crossing them off.

To break this cycle, focus on breaking down the monster list. I call it the "action ladder," where big, intimidating tasks are turned into tiny, concrete steps. So "Plan marketing campaign" turns into "Draft campaign goals," "List five target channels," "Research campaign budgets." Each rung is an action item that can be accomplished in 10 minutes or less, making it easier and less stressful to start.

Digital tools, when set up right, can help. With Notion or Asana, nest subtasks under broader goals and rearrange them visually, like turning chaos into a clear ladder you can climb. Use color, deadlines, and visual layouts to turn vague plans into actionable maps (Gelwicks, 2024). The point isn't aesthetic but clarity—helping your brain know exactly where to start.

Break the Cycle: Your Action Ladder Exercise

Take your current to-do list or open your favorite app. Pick one task you keep putting off. Write it at the top of a new page. Ask: "What's the very first small step I could take toward this?" Write that down. Then ask, "What next?" Break the task into at least three bite-sized actions, small enough to start right away. If a step remains unclear, break it down further.

Now move to Notion, Asana, or your tool of choice and create a new board or project, giving each step its own card or subtask. Assign a quick deadline for just the first action—ideally today.

If you find yourself rewriting your list or avoiding your action ladder again, briefly note what triggered your avoidance. Awareness is half the battle; clarity does the rest.

PERFECTIONISM PARALYSIS—WHEN "GOOD ENOUGH" FEELS IMPOSSIBLE

Some mornings, you might stare at your computer screen, fingers poised over the keyboard, heart racing as you try to start working on an important project. You want it to stand out. You want it to impress your boss, your team, and maybe even yourself. But then a tiny typo nags at you, or you second-guess a sentence, and suddenly you're stuck. Maybe you rewrite the same intro five times. Perhaps you never send the draft at all, telling yourself you'll return to it later, when it's "better." This is the perfectionist trap at work—the place where good enough feels like a personal failure, so nothing ever feels finished. For a content writer, this could look like endless tweaking of blog posts until deadlines slip past. In meetings, it's the urge to edit your own words before you even speak them out loud.

High standards can drive great results, but perfectionism is a different beast. High standards are about aiming for quality and growth—they push you to do your best with the time and resources you have. Perfectionism, on the other hand, whispers that anything less than flawless isn't worth showing at all. It's a voice that says, "Don't bother turning this in if there's one thing wrong." If you catch yourself hesitating to share work you've already revised several times or feeling anxious about feedback before anyone's even seen your draft, perfectionism might be calling the shots. Spotting this difference is critical. Are you editing because you see a clear, significant improvement or because you're afraid of being judged for missing something tiny?

The costs sneak up quietly but hit hard. That project you kept polishing? Someone else finished their version and got the recognition, while yours gathers digital dust. You might miss out on networking opportunities because your LinkedIn update never felt quite right. Burnout creeps in because endless editing is exhausting, and the constant loop of "not good enough" leaves little energy for new ideas. Even small daily tasks can stall: emails unsent, proposals hidden in draft folders, creative pitches left unspoken. The world moves ahead while you're still stuck on version fourteen of a single paragraph.

There's another way, one that invites a kinder rhythm into your workflow: minimum viable progress. This means asking not, "Is it perfect?" but "Is it ready enough to move forward?" This helps you shift your focus from flawless outcomes to forward motion. Picture yourself facing a stubborn task: an overdue report, a marketing plan, or a design comp that's lost its shine. Instead of aiming for 100%, ask, "What would this look like at 80% finished?" Most of the time, 80% is more than enough to get feedback, start a conversation, or move the project toward completion (Boyes, 2020).

Try using permission slips—simple scripts that free you from the chokehold of perfectionism. Write these down or say them out loud: "I am allowed to submit this draft for feedback before it's perfect." Or try: "This work is ready for review even if I see small flaws." The act of granting yourself permission lessens anxiety and teaches your brain that progress matters more than polish.

Next time you feel yourself spiraling—editing the same slide deck into the night or hesitating to send an important email—pause and name what's happening, "I'm stuck in perfectionism." Take one step toward minimum viable progress. Maybe it's sending a draft to a colleague with a note, "This is still rough, but I'd love your quick thoughts." Or perhaps it means scheduling ten minutes to review and send, then moving on without looking back.

If all else fails, ask yourself, what's the real risk if this isn't perfect? Most of the time, others won't even notice the details that keep you up at night. Making space for imperfection invites more feedback, learning, and momentum. It turns stalled projects into shared work and unshared ideas into real contributions.

Perfectionism may feel protective, but it often only shields you from growth and connection. Practicing "good enough" doesn't mean abandoning your standards—it means trusting that "done" is better than perfect when progress is what counts most. Give yourself room to show up as you are now, not just as some flawless version you imagine you need to be. That shift is where real productivity and relief begin.

DECISION FATIGUE AND THE TRAP OF TOO MANY CHOICES

There's something exhausting about a morning spent bouncing between options, even before you've checked off a single item on your list. You open your inbox, glance at Slack, and must immediately decide which message deserves your attention first. Maybe you're handed three new project management tools by your boss, all promising to revolutionize your workflow. Now, the pressure is on: pick Trello because you've used it before or Asana because your teammate swears by it? Suddenly, you're not really working at all—you're comparing features, reading reviews, and polling your group chat. The day slips away in a haze of tabs and second-guessing. That mental drain you feel isn't laziness; it's decision fatigue creeping in. Every micro-decision—what priority to tackle, which lunch to order, even what shirt to wear—chips away at your energy reserves. As choices pile up, fatigue settles in, and the likelihood of procrastination skyrockets—your mind just wants relief from the endless parade of "what now?"

At work, decision fatigue shows up everywhere, often disguised as productivity. You might spend twenty minutes debating which sales lead to call first out of a list of twenty names—the clock ticks by as you weigh client histories and try to predict outcomes. Or maybe you waste half an hour choosing between two almost identical PowerPoint templates for a client meeting. Each small fork in the road drains a little more motivation, making it harder to tackle the actual work ahead. Even lunch can become a mental slog if you're always choosing on the fly—should you get a salad from the café downstairs or takeout from that new Thai place? By the afternoon, your brain feels fried, and even simple tasks seem daunting.

The workplace often promotes choice as freedom, but too many options can paralyze rather than empower. If you feel like you're always making decisions but never moving forward, you're not alone. There's real science behind this drain: every choice—even minor ones

—uses up cognitive resources, leaving less willpower for important tasks later in the day (Braithwaite, n.d.). When your mind is over-loaded with low-stakes decisions, it starts to crave shortcuts or defaults. That's when procrastination sneaks in; you delay not because you don't care but because your brain can't handle another fork in the road.

The good news is that you don't have to live at the mercy of endless decisions. One powerful shift is building routines that automate repet-itive choices. For example, pre-setting your lunch orders for the week can spare you the dreaded 11:45 a.m. "What should I eat?" spiral. Choose your outfits for the week on Sunday night and free up that slice of mental energy each morning. Rely on default meeting templates or email responses for common requests instead of rein-venting the wheel every time. Setting these small defaults might sound trivial, but they add up—saving your brain for bigger challenges.

Another smart move is limiting options where possible. Give yourself three set time blocks for deep work and stick to them, rather than deciding each morning when to focus. If you're choosing between several tools or apps for a team project, pick one for a trial period and stick with it—resist the urge to compare endlessly. Create simple rules: always call the top three sales leads first thing in the morning; always use your favorite template unless there's truly a compelling reason to switch.

Self-Assessment: Spotting Decision Fatigue in Your Routine

Take a minute to reflect on your last workday. Where did you get stuck making choices? Did you find yourself comparing products, debating priorities, or researching small purchases far longer than needed? How did this impact your energy and motivation for bigger tasks? Write down three moments where indecision slowed you down or left you feeling drained. Look for patterns—are there certain times of day or types of decisions that trip you up more often? Awareness is your first defense against decision fatigue. Knowing where your willpower leaks makes it much easier to patch those holes and reclaim energy for what actually matters.

THE DISTRACTION DILEMMA: TECH, NOTIFICATIONS, AND ENVIRONMENT

You wake up, pour some coffee, and try to get a jump on your day. Perhaps you're working from a kitchen table or tucked away in a cubicle. Then, the first notification pings: Slack lights up with a random question from a coworker; Teams dings about an all-hands meeting; and your inbox fills up with "urgent" emails that look suspiciously like they could wait. You try to focus, but it feels like your attention is under attack from every direction. Each interruption pulls you out of what you're doing and dumps you back at square one. Even if you're a careful planner, these digital nudges add up. By noon, you might realize you've barely made progress on your most important work.

It's not just about tech, either. Your workspace itself can make or break your ability to pay attention. If you work in an open office, every cough, conversation, or footstep becomes another reason to look away from your screen. On video calls at home, kids banging on the door or the neighbor's leaf blower can break your rhythm. Even a phone face down next to the keyboard can wear down your willpower hour by hour.

Not all distractions are created equal, though. Some interruptions scream "urgent" but don't really matter, like a colleague's frantic chat about printer paper or a calendar pop-up for a meeting you could skip. These are the energy vampires of the modern office. Others are genuinely important—maybe your boss needs a quick answer that will help the entire team, or there's a real client emergency brewing. The tricky part is learning to spot the difference. Urgent distractions demand your attention right now, but often have a low impact in the long run. Important ones might not be noisy, but they move your priorities forward or save you pain later. If you react to everything as if it's urgent, you'll never have time for what's actually important.

This is where boundaries come into play—both digital and physical. Start by looking at the design of your workspace. If you can close a door, do it when you need to concentrate. Noise-canceling headphones can be a savior in busy environments. At home, even a visual cue like a "do not disturb" sign or a Post-it note can help signal to others that you're "heads-down." In open offices, carve out focus blocks by moving to quieter corners or booking small meeting rooms for solo work.

Digital boundaries are just as powerful. Most platforms have "do not disturb" settings—use them shamelessly to block space and time for deep work. Website blockers, like Freedom or StayFocused, can keep social media and news sites out of reach when you need to concentrate (Rosen et al., 2015). Turn off non-critical notifications on your phone and laptop and leave only true priority contacts able to reach you immediately. Batch-check Slack and email at set times instead of letting them dictate your attention all day.

If you want to get honest about what's stealing your focus, run a distraction audit. Take a typical day and log every time something interrupts your concentration: an email ping, a Slack message, someone walking by, or your own urge to check Instagram. Note the time and what broke your flow. After two days, review the list for patterns. Do certain apps cause most of your interruptions? Are there times when you're pulled away again and again? Use this information to tweak your environment and digital habits. Don't rely on your memory—seeing it in black and white makes change possible.

Personal Distraction Audit Checklist

- Track every interruption for two workdays (use the Notes app or plain paper).
- Mark if it was tech-related (Slack/Teams/email), environment-related (people/noise), or self-imposed (phone/social media).
- Decide if it was urgent, important, neither, or both?
- Highlight repeat offenders: apps, times of day, and specific coworkers.
- Set one new boundary tomorrow: mute notifications for 1 hour, close the office door, or use headphones.
- Revisit the audit after one week to see what has changed and what still needs work.

Small tweaks in how you handle digital clutter, set up your workspace, or manage interruptions can mean the difference between constant frustration and actually getting into flow on tasks that matter most. Sometimes, your brain just needs less noise so it can finally settle into the work in front of you.

Want a more structured approach? If you're ready to get serious about identifying and eliminating your biggest focus killers, check out the personal distraction audit tool located on our resource hub. This detailed tracker will help you discover when, why, and how often you get interrupted—plus give you a clear action plan for taking back control of your attention.

Use the link here: https://bit.ly/MyDistractionAudit

Or use this QR code:

GUILT, SHAME, AND THE SELF-CRITICISM SPIRAL

You put off a project. You miss a deadline, or maybe you never send that email sitting in your draft folder. At first, it's just a flicker of discomfort—an uneasy feeling in your stomach. But then the floodgates open. You start replaying what you did (or didn't do) in your mind. The self-talk gets loud: "Why can't I just do this like everyone else? What's wrong with me? I always mess things up." That's how procrastination quietly becomes something heavier. It's not just about being late or behind anymore. It's about feeling like you failed and then beating yourself up for it, which only makes things worse the next time you try to start a similar task.

That loop of guilt and shame isn't just unpleasant—it makes procrastination harder to break. Self-blame feels like it should motivate you, but it rarely does. Instead, it drains your energy, eats at your confidence, and leaves you feeling isolated. The more you criticize yourself, the more anxiety you feel about starting again. It becomes easier to avoid your work because facing it means facing those harsh inner voices. It's a trap that pulls you in deeper with every cycle: delay leads to guilt, which grows into shame, which then makes action feel impossible.

There's a real difference between healthy self-reflection and destructive self-criticism. Healthy reflection looks at what happened and asks honest questions, "What got in my way? What might I try differently next time?" It comes from a desire to learn, not punish. Destructive self-criticism, though, is a barrage of "shoulds" and feelings of "never enough." It turns a single missed deadline into a sweeping judgment about your worth. The language shifts from "I missed this task" to "I'm just lazy" or "I'm not cut out for this." That shift is subtle but powerful. Healthy reflection moves you forward—self-criticism freezes you in place.

Guilt and shame don't just live in your head; they have physical effects, too. You might notice your shoulders tense up, your stomach twist, or even your sleep gets disrupted after a day of beating yourself up. All of this makes resilience—the ability to bounce back and try again—so much harder. Shame whispers that you're alone in this, that everyone else has it together, and that if you reveal your struggle, you'll be exposed as a fraud. None of that is true, but those feelings are convincing—and deeply draining.

There's a way out of this spiral, and it starts with self-compassion. You may roll your eyes at the idea at first, especially if you're used to being tough on yourself. But self-compassion means treating yourself with the same basic kindness you'd give to anyone else in your shoes—not letting yourself off the hook or making excuses. It's pausing when you start to hear those negative voices and asking yourself, "Would I talk to a friend like this?" If the answer is no, you probably need to dial back the criticism and turn up the support.

A simple way to practice this is with self-kindness journaling. After a slip-up or missed deadline, instead of stewing in regret or handing out your own mental punishments, grab a notebook or open your notes app. Write a letter to yourself as if you were comforting a close friend who's struggling with the same problem. Start with what happened; be honest but gentle. Then write what you wish someone would say to you right now, "You tried your best under tough circumstances. One mistake doesn't define you. It's okay to feel frustrated." Give yourself permission to feel disappointed without spiraling into shame (Neff, n.d.).

Another helpful tool is guided reflection. When guilt flares up, pause and ask, "If my friend told me this story, what would I say?" Maybe you'd remind them that everyone misses deadlines sometimes, or that starting is always hard after a setback. Perhaps you'd help them see all the things they did accomplish instead of focusing on what they failed to. The act of shifting perspective—stepping outside your head and into someone else's shoes—softens the internal pressure and opens the door for real growth.

Self-compassion doesn't erase accountability; it makes it possible to try again without fear. The next time guilt starts to gnaw at you after procrastinating, notice how quickly shame tries to take over. Interrupt it with a moment of kindness—just one gentle thought or sentence is enough to change the tone. Over time, these small acts of grace build resilience and help break the cycle that keeps procrastination playing on repeat. We'll explore self-compassion practices in greater detail in Chapter 8.

THE FEAR OF FEEDBACK—HOW CRITICISM KEEPS YOU STUCK

Few things stall progress faster than the dread of someone picking apart your hard work. Sometimes, it feels safer to stay in the editing phase forever rather than risk hearing, "This isn't quite right." You probably know the scenario—a designer fiddles with colors and fonts until the proposal is overdue, not because the work lacks merit but because the thought of a client's negative comments stings more than another late night. Even in less creative roles, fear of feedback can be paralyzing. You might hesitate to send a project update to your boss because you're convinced you'll miss something obvious. Or maybe you avoid pitching a new idea in meetings because you're worried it'll be shot down. This anxiety isn't just uncomfortable; it's a huge driver of procrastination.

The mind often magnifies the threat of criticism, making every review feel like a judgment on your worth. However, not all feedback is created equal. There's a world of difference between constructive feedback, which aims to help you grow, and destructive feedback, which tears down without offering a path forward. Constructive feedback sounds like, "Try adding more detail to this section," or "Your main point is strong—clarify it with an example." Destructive feedback is vague or personal, such as comments like "This doesn't make sense" or "I expected better." Learning to spot the difference helps you react with less fear. When you receive feedback that stings, ask yourself: Is this showing me how to improve, or is it just someone venting? If it's the former, there's value—even if it hurts at first.

It took me years to see feedback as something other than a threat. Early in my career, I'd edit emails for half an hour before pressing send, dreading every typo someone might catch. Eventually, though, I noticed the most successful people around me weren't waiting for perfect—they were sharing early drafts and inviting quick reactions. A marketing specialist I once worked with had a habit that changed my outlook: she'd send her presentation slides to a mentor before they were finished and ask for just one thing to improve. This small request focused the feedback and made it feel doable, not overwhelming. Instead of hearing a laundry list of flaws, she'd receive targeted advice, such as "Try tightening slide three" or "Add a stat to support your intro." Her projects moved faster, and her confidence grew. The fear faded as she realized most feedback wasn't personal, just practical.

If opening yourself up to critique feels impossible, try shifting your mindset. Feedback is just data—a tool for refining your work, not a verdict on your value. You can even practice getting comfortable with it using what I call a "feedback exposure ladder." Start with low-stakes situations: share something minor—a draft email or a social media caption—with someone you trust. Ask them for one specific suggestion instead of general notes. Once you're comfortable there, move up a rung: maybe share an early version of a report with a supportive peer or ask for input on your meeting notes from a colleague. Gradually work toward more public or high-stakes feedback situations, like presenting unfinished work in a team meeting or submitting a rough draft to your manager. Each step helps desensitize you to the discomfort while building resilience.

Taking this approach redefines criticism as something survivable—and even useful. The more often you seek input before perfection, the more you realize that most people want to help you improve rather than tear you down. With each round of feedback you survive (and maybe even appreciate), the less power your old fears have. Eventually, the cycle shifts—you start projects knowing that feedback is part of the process, not something to dread at the finish line.

As we close this chapter, remember that procrastination feeds on the fear of messiness, mistakes, and especially critique. Now, you've seen how triggers like feedback anxiety can quietly take control of your productivity. Understanding these obstacles gives you power over them. In the next chapter, we'll start building real strategies for action —so you're not just aware of your triggers—you're ready to move past them for good.

CHAPTER 3
QUICK WINS—GETTING STARTED WHEN YOU FEEL STUCK

THE "2-MINUTE RULE" FOR INSTANT MOMENTUM

There's a weird sense of inertia that creeps in when you stare at your screen, knowing there's a heap of work to do, but you're not sure where to start. Sometimes, your mind tells you that if you can't finish the whole thing right now, it's pointless even to begin. That's when the "2-Minute Rule" becomes a game-changer. Rather than tricking yourself with grand plans or hyping yourself up for a productivity marathon, this rule focuses on lowering the bar until getting started barely feels like effort. The idea is simple: if you can take action on something in two minutes or less, do it immediately (Clear, n.d.). But even more important, the rule opens a backdoor for momentum. Instead of fixating on the finish line, you focus on just showing up.

Starting small interrupts procrastination's favorite excuse—overwhelm. Your brain likes easy wins, and the two-minute entry point is so low-pressure that resistance has nowhere to hide. This isn't just about efficiency; it's about reprogramming how you relate to tasks. When you begin with a minuscule step, you bypass the internal friction and anxiety that usually keep you frozen. Tiny actions create micro-victories, and these micro-victories trick your brain into thinking, "Well, if I can do this, maybe I can keep going." The goal isn't to finish everything at once, but simply to nudge yourself into motion and let momentum carry you forward.

Think about your day—the endless swirl of work demands, home responsibilities, and those nagging chores that never seem urgent enough to tackle but always hang in the background. There are dozens of tasks that fit the 2-minute window. At work, this could be replying to a single email that's been haunting your inbox, drafting the subject line for that overdue report, or glancing over your meeting notes and jotting down just one action item. At home, maybe it's laying out your workout clothes for tomorrow morning, loading just a few dishes into the dishwasher, or texting a quick thank-you to a friend. These aren't glamorous moves, but they break the cycle of stalling out before you even begin.

You might catch yourself thinking, "This is too small to matter." But here's the truth: getting started is more powerful than waiting for perfect conditions. When the bar is low, you don't need heroic motivation or a burst of inspiration. You just need to do something—anything—right now. It's a psychological hack that leverages what's called a "gateway habit"—an easy action that opens the door to bigger habits down the line (Clear, n.d.). The more you flex this habit-building muscle, the more automatic it becomes.

If you want to experiment with the 2-Minute Rule in real life, ask yourself: "What's the smallest piece of this I can do right now?" If you're staring at an intimidating project proposal, maybe all you do is open the file and write a working title. If your apartment is a mess, start by tossing one piece of junk mail in the trash. Are you facing a stack of unread emails? Reply to one critical follow-up message or dash off a three-word message: "Let's schedule this." These tiny actions are like pushing a snowball down a hill—once it moves, it keeps rolling.

Scripts and prompts can make this easier when your mind tries to bargain with you or distract you with alternative plans. Try these:

- "What would be so easy right now that I couldn't say no?"
- "If I only had two minutes before my next meeting, what could I move forward?"
- "What tiny action would make the next step easier?"
- "How can I make progress without committing to finishing?"

Let me share a real example from someone who put this into practice. A marketing manager I coached struggled with starting campaign proposals—each one felt massive and make-or-break. Instead of aiming to finish in one sitting (which never happened), she adopted the 2-Minute Rule by committing only to writing a subject line and saving the file with the campaign title. This took less than two minutes but made the project feel real, bite-sized, and doable. And most days, she'd catch herself adding a few bullet points or jotting down a headline idea before she realized it. The difference wasn't in her ability or time—it was about lowering her resistance to starting.

Another case: a remote analyst who hated daily reports turned things around by using the rule to open the previous day's spreadsheet and shade one cell based on performance before doing anything else. That single click broke his hesitation loop, and he would often update more data or write a quick summary because starting felt safe and manageable.

2-Minute Quick Wins Checklist

Use this as a menu of instant starters for work and home:

- Reply "Received, thank you" to an email
- Type a first draft subject line for any report or proposal
- Lay out workout gear by your bed
- Text your partner what time you'll be home
- Open your task app and tick off one completed item
- Jot down three words as an outline for an upcoming meeting
- Place one dirty dish in the dishwasher

- Send a calendar invite for a future call
- Write one sentence in your project doc
- Schedule tomorrow's lunch on your phone

The real value isn't in crossing off tiny tasks; it's in teaching yourself that motion beats perfection. Small steps build trust in yourself, and that trust grows into momentum far beyond what force or willpower ever could muster.

EAT THE FROG: CONQUERING THE HARDEST TASK FIRST

Every morning, whether you realize it or not, you make a deal with yourself about how the day will go. Some days, you wake up, and the first thing on your mind is that one task you absolutely do not want to face. Maybe it's making a difficult phone call to a client, giving constructive feedback to a colleague, or starting a complex spreadsheet you've been dreading all week. That's your "frog"—the task that's so unappealing or anxiety-inducing that you'd rather do almost anything else. The idea behind "Eat the Frog" is straightforward: if you tackle your biggest, scariest, or most annoying job first, everything after that feels lighter. This isn't just motivational fluff. When you handle the hardest thing right away, you unlock a surge of mental energy and focus that seeps into the rest of your day. You stop wasting willpower on avoidance and get real, tangible relief once it's done.

Your frog might look different from mine or anyone else's. For some, it's a call to an unhappy customer or an overdue performance review with your team. Others find their frog is working on a pitch deck that's been hanging over them for weeks or scheduling a doctor's appointment they've been putting off. Sometimes, your frog is something deeply personal, like sitting down with your partner for a tough conversation about money or setting boundaries with someone at work. It's always the task that creates the most resistance in your mind and drains your motivation just thinking about it. The trick is to recognize it before you get swept up in its disruptive power.

Identifying your frog takes honest self-inquiry. You can use a simple prioritization checklist to pinpoint which task deserves the "frog" label today. Ask yourself: what have I been avoiding the longest? Which item on my list makes me tense up or sigh out loud? Which unfinished thing would leave me breathing easier if I could just get it off my plate before noon? If the thought of finishing it makes you feel instantly lighter, that's probably your frog—write it down. Don't let vague guilt hover in the background; naming it gives you power over it.

Once you know your frog, set up your morning to face it head-on and build a routine that makes tackling it almost automatic. First, block out thirty minutes on your calendar before doing anything else—before opening email, before checking Slack, before scrolling through news feeds. This is your "frog block." Next, write it on your schedule, put your phone out of reach, and silence notifications so nothing can chip away at your focus. The less noise around you, the harder it is for avoidance to sneak in.

Making preparations to eat your frog helps even more if procrastination usually wins. Lower friction to start by prepping what you need the night before: leave the report template open on your desktop, jot down three talking points for that awkward call, or stack any related paperwork next to your laptop so it's immediately accessible when you sit down. The fewer decisions you have to make at the moment, the less likely you are to bail. If you're working from home and distractions are everywhere, tell people in your space you're unavailable for those blocked thirty minutes. Consider putting a sticky note on your door or sending a text to housemates so they respect your focus time.

The first few times you try this, expect discomfort. You might feel fidgety or even irritable, like every cell in your body wants to check email or do something "productive" instead. That's normal. You're rewiring old avoidance patterns. Remind yourself that discomfort is temporary, but relief lasts all day. Once you start, focus only on progress, not perfection. If you can't finish the whole task in one sitting, break it down: send that first draft, make the first call, or tackle the most stressful piece first (George, 2023).

There's a reason this approach changes lives. I recall speaking with an HR lead who used to dread performance review season so much that she'd spend hours tweaking templates and responding to low-priority emails just to avoid having feedback conversations. After committing to eating her frog first thing each morning, blocking thirty minutes for her toughest reviews, she found that her anxiety dropped off as soon as she finished that first meeting each day. Not only did her afternoons become less stressful, but she also started looking forward to getting things checked off her list instead of dreading them.

Another story that sticks with me is of a sales rep at a tech startup who hated making cold calls so much that he'd push them until late afternoon and then rush through them with zero energy or confidence. When he switched to scheduling his frog block right after his morning coffee—before he even opened his inbox—he noticed two things: he was more relaxed on those calls, and his daily sales numbers improved because he wasn't distracted by dreading them all day.

If you want a powerful boost of self-trust and momentum, eat your frog before anything else has a chance to drain your willpower. The mental space and pride you gain from conquering what scares you most first thing can ripple into every corner of your day—turning even the hardest weeks into something more manageable.

BRAIN DUMP TO BREAK THE FREEZE

Some days, your mind feels like a closet stuffed so full you can barely close the door. Thoughts pile up, worries swirl, random to-dos float in and out, and beneath it all, there's a low hum of anxiety that refuses to switch off. When you're paralyzed by all that noise, getting started on anything feels impossible. That's where brain dumping comes in—a fast, cathartic method to unload mental clutter and snap out of analysis paralysis. Unlike a regular to-do list, which forces you to organize, prioritize, and structure tasks, a brain dump is intentionally disorganized and messy. There's no order or ranking. You just pour out whatever is sitting in your head—big, small, significant, silly—until your mind feels lighter.

The magic of a brain dump is its lack of rules. You don't need to filter or judge what comes out. You might jot down "Call dentist," "Ask for a raise," "Buy oat milk," "Figure out spreadsheet formulas," or "Why did

I say that in last week's meeting?". You're not aiming for a polished masterpiece or even a neat checklist—you're just clearing your head so you can see what's actually weighing you down. That release alone can thaw the freeze that keeps you stuck.

You can brain dump anywhere, using any method. If you love digital tools, open a blank Google Doc or Notion page and set a timer for five minutes. Type whatever pops into your mind—don't censor yourself. If you're more tactile, grab a notebook or the back of an old receipt and start writing without lifting your pen. Some people prefer sticky notes so they can move ideas around later. Others use voice memos while driving or walking. The medium doesn't matter—what counts is the act of unloading. For people who spend their days bouncing between tech and meetings, digital options are great because you can copy, paste, and sort later. But there's something satisfying about seeing messy scribbles fill up a physical page, too.

Try this template if you're new to the process: at the top of your page, write "Brain Dump—No Order." Set a five-minute timer. Then ask yourself: what's nagging at me right now? What am I avoiding? What decisions are hanging over my head? What random thoughts keep popping up? Dump it all out, even if it sounds ridiculous or trivial. Don't stop writing until the timer goes off. Resist the urge to tidy up as you go—this is about release, not perfection.

After you finish, you'll probably have a chaotic list, with some items being urgent tasks and others just mental noise that's been bugging you for weeks. This is where transformation begins. Start by grabbing two highlighters or using colored tags in your digital doc. Highlight anything that feels like a "quick win" (stuff you could do with little effort) in one color, maybe responding to an email, making a call, or setting up a lunch with a coworker. Use another color for larger or long-term projects—the ones that require more planning or multiple steps. Now, you've turned chaos into two clear categories: tasks you can complete today and tasks that require more time.

The next phase involves moving these items from the raw dump to the action system. Drag or copy quick wins into your main task manager or calendar—whatever tool works for you. Don't overload yourself;

aim for just two or three quick wins per day so you don't set yourself up for failure. For the larger projects, break them down into smaller pieces (more on that in the next section). Some people find it helpful to add deadlines or group big tasks by context ("work," "home," or "personal growth") so they don't feel overwhelmed.

I've heard from many knowledge workers who swear by brain dumping as their secret weapon against overwhelm. One project manager at a fast-paced tech company told me he used to wake up every Monday feeling like he was already behind—unanswered emails, unplanned meetings, half-formed creative ideas that never got started. He began doing a five-minute brain dump every morning, first thing, before opening his inbox. This ritual let him spot small tasks he could finish fast and cleared enough mental space that he could focus during his meetings instead of stressing about forgotten details.

Another friend—a parent juggling freelance work from home—shared how brain dumping helped her survive days when everything seemed urgent at once. She'd list out every single worry and chore: requests from clients, reminders from her kid's school, groceries she kept forgetting, even doubts about her work performance. Out of the mess, she'd pull three things for that day and let go of the rest until tomorrow, finally able to breathe without the constant weight of guilt.

The biggest gift of brain dumping is relief—it lets you see that your mind doesn't have to hold everything at once. Once your thoughts are on paper (or screen), they stop swirling in circles and start becoming problems you can solve (Chen, 2024).

MICRO-TASKS: SLICING PROJECTS INTO ACTIONABLE STEPS

You know that paralyzed feeling when an impossibly big and vague project stares back from your list? You keep shifting it from one week to the next, hoping you'll suddenly wake up motivated enough to tackle it in one heroic burst. The truth is that day almost never comes. The bigger and fuzzier the project, the more your brain protests. Even if you're motivated, you might end up circling around the task, rearranging your space, or working on something else just to avoid that heavy sense of overwhelm. Here's where micro-tasking flips your experience. Instead of wrestling with "Write an annual report," you dissect it into tiny, hyper-clear steps, like "open the report template," "jot down three bullet points for the introduction," and "pull sales numbers from last quarter." Each slice is so specific that it's hard to talk yourself out of starting.

As we saw in Chapter 2, traditional to-do lists pile on the pressure with vague, overwhelming tasks: "Prep presentation," "Update website," "Plan event." These lists may look productive, but they rarely move you forward. You end up with a backlog of aspirations, not actions. Micro-tasking, on the other hand, is all about clarity and progress. It's like swapping out a 10,000-piece puzzle for smaller piles of completed corners and edges. Each micro-task—no matter how small—gives your mind a clear direction and a sense of control. Momentum grows when you cross off specifics, not when you stare at mountains.

Let's get practical. Imagine you're a remote employee facing a quarterly presentation that has been looming over your head for weeks. The classic way to handle this task would be to write "finish Q2 presentation" in your planner and hope for a spark of motivation. But watch what happens when you break it down:

1. Open last quarter's slide deck
2. Copy last quarter's title slide and update for Q2
3. List five bullet points for the introduction
4. Pull sales data from the team's Google Drive
5. Paste in one chart for revenue trends
6. Draft two talking points for each main section
7. Find a quote from your boss's last email
8. Save everything and close the file

Instead of one giant task, now you have eight micro-tasks—each one doable, each one with a clear finish line. You can even spread these steps over several days if your schedule is chaotic or if deep focus time is hard to come by. The beauty is that every small action is a mini win that pushes you forward and chips away at resistance.

A worksheet or digital template can make this easier, especially if you lean on visual tools in your daily workflow. Try using a Kanban board —either in Trello, Notion, or even on sticky notes stuck to your wall. Create three columns: To Do, Doing, Done. Write each micro-task on its own card or note and place it initially in the "To Do" column. Move it across the board as your work progresses. Watching cards pile up in the "Done" column is strangely satisfying because it provides proof that real progress is happening, even if the project isn't finished yet (Boogaard, 2019). We'll dive deeper into Kanban boards in Chapter 4.

If digital tools aren't your thing, grab a piece of paper and draw three columns by hand. List every single step you can think of—no matter how tiny—in the "To Do" column, move it to the "Doing" column, and then the "Done" column as you complete each step. There's something powerful about seeing progress in motion; it turns abstract effort into visible achievement.

Don't overlook the importance of celebrating when you complete a micro-task, either. Productivity isn't just about getting things done; it's about training your brain to expect rewards for action. Every time you finish a step, pause for a second and give yourself a small win: check it off your app, slap a sticker on your template, or just say "done" out loud. (It may sound silly, but it works.) Some people set up digital confetti animations in their project management tools or play a favorite song as they move through tasks.

Another helpful trick is using a Pomodoro timer for each micro-task— set it for 25 minutes and see how many steps you can finish before the bell rings (Lmay, n.d.). Even if you only finish one or two steps, that's more progress than another day lost to avoidance. We'll explore the Pomodoro technique in greater detail in Chapter 4.

You'll notice that as your list of micro-tasks shrinks, so does your stress level. Instead of facing a looming monster, you're just taking the next small bite—and then another. Each card or step moved, check made, or celebratory pause is proof that you're not stuck; you're moving forward at your own pace.

Sometimes, I'll take things further and break steps into sub-steps if I'm really feeling stuck. If "draft first paragraph" feels like too much, I'll write "type one sentence" as its own micro-task. No step is too small if it gets you started and keeps resistance at bay.

Reflection helps solidify this habit. After finishing a project with micro-tasking, look back at your worksheet or Kanban board and notice how each tiny win built real momentum. Instead of giving you one more productivity hack, this changes the way you approach big projects forever. The next time something feels overwhelming, remember: you don't have to climb the whole mountain today. Just take the next step that's right in front of you and celebrate each bit of progress, one micro-task at a time.

THE "START RITUAL": DESIGNING YOUR PERSONALIZED LAUNCH SEQUENCE

Often, the hardest part of getting work done is simply crossing the line from not working to actually working. There's a strange limbo—almost like stage fright—where you know you should begin but can't seem to shift gears. A "start ritual" can make all the difference. It acts as your personal launch sequence: a short, repeatable routine that signals your brain that it's time to focus. Forget superstition—this works because consistent cues turn starting into a habit, not a battle.

Start rituals work by anchoring you in the present and preparing you to focus. Perhaps it's brewing coffee and savoring its warmth, slipping on noise-canceling headphones and playing a focus playlist, or lighting a candle before opening your laptop. The magic lies in engaging your senses—sight, touch, sound, smell—so your brain connects those specific cues with deep work. Especially if you work from home and struggle to separate work from daily life, these anchors help draw a (mental) line between the chaos outside and your productive zone inside.

Building a start ritual isn't complicated or time-consuming. Begin by noticing what sensory cues help you feel alert or centered, like the scratch of a pen, the hum of a white noise app, or stretching your arms.

Pair this action with your first work step, such as taking three deep breaths, tidying your desk, or placing a favorite mug nearby. These small moves quickly become reliable triggers for your brain to shift into work mode.

Muscle memory matters here, too. If you always start by opening a specific app, make that the first thing you touch. Or open a blank document and type the date. These aren't just routines; they're neural shortcuts that train your mind to expect focus after your ritual. Habit shapes behavior more than motivation, and repeating your ritual saves energy you'd otherwise waste on resistance.

Professionals use start rituals in unique ways—there's no one-size-fits-all. A designer lights a citrus candle before opening creative software, signaling it's time for design (not emails). For a remote worker juggling roles, a daily routine of arranging notebooks and playing a work-only playlist does the trick. Parents working from home might need an even more intentional transition. One dad uses a five-minute guided meditation after school drop-off, creating a clear mental shift from parenting to work.

Other rituals are movement-based. One woman stretches for two minutes at her desk before Zoom meetings, waking up both body and mind. A freelance consultant does ten jumping jacks in his home office before settling into deep work sessions, using the physical activity to shift his energy and signal focus time.

If you haven't tried a start ritual, experiment for a week. Pick a sensory cue—sound, scent, touch—and pair it with your work start. Keep it short and repeat it daily, adjusting as needed to find what feels natural and effective. Your ritual might look different from someone else's, and that's perfectly fine. What matters is that it helps you cut through hesitation and begin.

Start rituals aren't magic; they use solid behavioral science. They anchor new habits by giving your brain a reliable routine, so it knows what comes next. You don't have to rely solely on sheer willpower—the ritual provides a reassuring, predictable start. Over time, starting work stops feeling like a huge uphill battle.

Try This: Design Your Start Ritual

Identify something in your pre-work routine that helps you feel relaxed or energized—pouring tea, dimming lights, playing an upbeat song—and link it directly to the first step of your work task for five days in a row. After a few repetitions, notice how you feel. Adjust if needed and keep it simple.

The secret to getting started isn't pushing harder—it's creating signals that make crossing the starting line easier each day. These small rituals lay the groundwork for bigger strategies ahead, helping you maintain momentum no matter how hectic your schedule becomes.

CHAPTER 4
BUILDING YOUR ANTI-PROCRASTINATION TOOLKIT

HOW TO USE KANBAN BOARDS AND VISUAL PROGRESS TRACKERS

Ever notice how checking something off a list gives you a rush? That's because your brain is wired to love visuals. When you see progress mapped out—sticky notes on a board or digital cards sliding into the "Done" column—you get a genuine boost. Visual cues activate your reward system, making challenging projects feel doable and concrete. You aren't just guessing at your progress; you're watching it happen. Studies back this up: when you visually track your workflow, your mind identifies bottlenecks, notices achievements, and releases dopamine with each milestone (Gelwicks, 2024). That's why visual task management tools, such as Kanban boards, can break cycles of overwhelm and stagnation.

Kanban boards provide much-needed clarity. At their simplest, they have columns representing work stages, with each task on its own card. As you make progress, you move cards from left to right. To set up a physical board, use sticky notes on a wall or a whiteboard and create columns labeled "To Do," "In Progress," "Waiting," and "Done." One task goes on each sticky note, placed in "To Do." As you work, move the notes through each stage. Instantly, you can see what needs tackling, what's in progress or on hold, and what's finished. Prefer digital? Tools like Trello, Notion, or Asana work similarly. Open a new board, create columns, add your tasks as cards, and move them step-by-step as you complete tasks.

Customization and Flexibility

Kanban's real power lies in flexibility. If you juggle multiple projects, color-code cards for quick priority checks: blue for client work, yellow for administrative tasks, and green for personal goals. In team environments, assign cards with avatars or initials. Use a "Waiting" column to keep tabs on tasks held up by others. For hybrid lives, divide your board into sections for work and personal so everything is visible and organized by context.

Progress Trackers and Gamifying Productivity

Progress trackers add a dose of fun, keep you accountable, and are much more effective than simple lists. Think of sticking stars on a calendar for workouts or collecting digital badges for completed tasks. Every win—big or small—is worth celebrating. These quick rewards aren't childish; they tap directly into your motivation system (Abdaal, 2024). Progress becomes a visible, rewarding game, with constant encouragement to move forward.

Real-Life Kanban Board Setups

Consider a marketing campaign column with headings such as "Ideas," "Content in Progress," "Review," and "Published." As projects transition from draft to live, the path is visible, and the process remains organized. At home, a board could have labels for "To Buy," "Assembling," "Waiting for Delivery," and "Complete," with each family member using colored notes to track their progress. Freelancers might track "Potential Leads," "Contacted," "In Negotiation," "Work Started," and "Invoice Sent," providing a clear overview of revenue flow and next steps.

Interactive Exercise: Build Your First Kanban Board

Spend fifteen minutes with sticky notes and a board or jump into Trello (or another tool). Set up "To Do," "In Progress," and "Done" columns. Write down every open task—work, home, or side projects—and place them in "To Do." As you begin a task, move it to "In Progress," and when finished, move it to "Done." At week's end, check the "Done" column and celebrate all progress, big or small. Seeing your completed tasks will inform and remind you that progress is real and built continuously.

Moving tasks across your Kanban board is surprisingly satisfying and can quickly switch your thinking from overwhelmed to in control. Each colorful step forward is proof to your brain that you're making progress.

TIME-BLOCKING THAT WORKS (FOR REAL SCHEDULES)

Time-blocking is one of those rare productivity methods that gives you back control, even if your days are packed with meetings, random requests, or last-minute surprises. Forget rigid routines that crumble when life throws you a curveball; this approach is all about carving out space for what matters most while still leaving room for the unpredictable. Think of it as a living blueprint for your week, where you decide what deserves your best focus—and when. It's less about micromanaging every minute and more about protecting your priorities from the chaos of everyone else's demands. You start by looking at the week ahead and sketching out blocks of time for different types of work. Maybe you reserve "Deep Work" in the morning for heads-down projects, like report writing or coding. Later, you schedule an "Admin Power Hour" to bulldoze through emails, forms, or logistics. Don't forget to block "Lunch/Reset" breaks for actual breathing room and toss in a "Creative Jam" session for brainstorming or content creation. Color-coding these blocks in your digital calendar can make them pop and give you a quick visual check of how balanced (or overloaded) your week looks.

Time blocks aren't just handy for work, though. Make sure you first block out personal time, whether that's a mid-afternoon walk, school pickup, or a quiet thirty minutes to read. Treating those moments as non-negotiable helps you preserve your energy. Once you've blocked personal priorities, block out recurring commitments—weekly team meetings, recurring check-ins, or standing appointments. Next, identify where deep work can fit; maybe it's two-hour chunks early in the week before your calendar fills up with calls. For admin tasks, batch them together in a single block to avoid spreading them across your day.

Inevitably, real life will crash into your plan: meetings run over, a surprise request pops up, someone calls in sick and you have to cover their shift. To stay sane, build in buffer blocks—what I call "white space"—between meetings or after major projects. These floating zones aren't wasted time; they're breathing room for catching up, pivoting, or recovering after a tough stretch. When interruptions hit, don't toss out your whole plan. Instead, use a quick rescheduling hack: drag the missed block to another open slot or split it into two smaller sessions if needed. If your "Deep Work" block gets eaten by a fire drill, move it to tomorrow morning and protect it fiercely.

Digital tools make time blocking much easier to manage and adjust on the fly. Open Google Calendar and create recurring blocks labeled by task type—"Deep Work," "Admin," "Lunch/Reset," "Meetings," and "Creative Jam." Use different colors for quick scanning and drag to rearrange when priorities shift. Outlook works just as well, especially with its category tags and color-coded events, and Notion lovers can design custom schedule databases with linked tasks that update as you go. If you're visual, try splitting your calendar into horizontal rows—one for work, one for personal—to see the full spread of your commitments.

To help you get started, here's a sample weekly planning worksheet idea: on Sunday night or Monday morning, list out your three top priorities for the week. Then look at your calendar and mark blocks where each priority can live. Fill in meetings and scheduled appointments next. Add buffer zones after any block longer than two hours. Reserve 30–60 minutes each Friday to review what worked and shuffle things around for next week. If you're a remote worker juggling work and family, screenshot your calendar to use as a reference when negotiating new requests or fending off interruptions.

With time-blocking, you're not trying to cram more into each day—you're making room to focus more deeply, one block at a time. With practice, it becomes second nature to safeguard those blocks from busy work or interruptions. You'll find yourself finishing more of the right things—with less stress—because you planned space for both deep work and life's curveballs (Scroggs, 2024).

TASK BATCHING TO MINIMIZE CONTEXT SWITCHING

Ever get that mental whiplash after bouncing between emails, spreadsheets, and client calls all within one hour? That's normal. Our brains aren't designed for rapid context-switching between tasks. Task batching solves this by grouping similar tasks so you can complete them in focused stretches. It's like running all your errands in one trip instead of darting back and forth across town. The benefit is huge because every task switch leads to "attention residue," a loss of focus that can take up to 20 minutes to regain with each occurrence. With multiple distractions daily, your energy can be sapped quickly, and your day can feel wasted.

Batching eliminates this scattered feeling. By answering emails only at set times or doing all your calls in a single window, your mind settles into a productive groove. You'll work faster and make fewer mistakes since you're not dividing your attention. For example, instead of checking your inbox every ten minutes, establish two or three time slots: after breakfast, after lunch, and before wrapping up. This shields you from constant notifications and helps you reclaim lost time. When scheduling meetings, consider grouping them all in a single afternoon (perhaps on a Wednesday) to minimize interruptions to your creative work. At home, handle bills and paperwork in one session instead of spreading them throughout the week.

Some tasks are more suited to batching than others. Repetitive or administrative tasks (emails, calendar updates, expense reports) are ideal for batching. Creative or complex work (writing, designing, problem-solving) usually requires uninterrupted focus, so block out separate, distraction-free time for these. For unexpected tasks, keep a running list to address them during a separate batch instead of breaking your flow right away.

Creating an effective batch schedule requires intention. Start by listing your weekly routine tasks—work and personal. Mark, which ones are most draining when interrupted. Then, group similar tasks, such as emails, calls, research, and errands. Assign each batch a specific time slot in your calendar, such as Mondays for creative work, Wednesdays for meetings, and Fridays for administrative tasks. If balancing a busy job and home life, batch chores on Saturday or meal prep on Sunday afternoons (Laoyan, 2025).

Use scripts and tools to safeguard your batch sessions. If someone asks for a meeting outside your set window, say, "I take calls after 2 p.m. on Wednesdays—does that work?" Set an email autoresponder: "I check email at 10 a.m., 1 p.m., and 4 p.m.—if urgent, text me." This helps others know when to expect a reply and relieves you of the pressure to respond instantly. For regular tasks or themed days, tape a checklist to your workspace: "Monday: Content. Tuesday: Team. Thursday: Projects. Friday: Admin." This helps to protect your batches from constant interruptions.

If your job resists fixed routines, try theming work blocks. Make afternoons "Focus Blocks" for deep work, mornings for administrative tasks, or schedule a "Power Hour" daily for whichever batch needs it most. For teams, encourage everyone to try batching so meetings and requests don't constantly interrupt each other's focused work time.

Task batching works at home, too. Group errands in one outing (bank, dry cleaner, post office) rather than spreading them out. Do grocery shopping in one trip. With meal prep, batch tasks by chopping all vegetables together or cooking proteins to cover several days at once.

After a week of batching, reflect on what improved and which interruptions lingered. Adjust your windows or add buffer time as needed. With practice, batching will feel natural, and your days will become clearer, less fragmented, and more productive—even when surprises crop up.

POMODORO TECHNIQUE—CUSTOMIZING SPRINTS FOR YOUR ENERGY

The Pomodoro Technique breaks your work into short, focused sprints, followed by set rest periods. Standard practice involves using a 25-minute timer for focused work on a single task, followed by a 5-minute break. After four sprints, you take a longer pause of 15–20 minutes for a deeper reset. This isn't just about discipline; it works with your mind's natural attention rhythms. As the timer counts down, the urge to check your phone or wander fades, replaced by the drive to push through and finish the sprint. The finish line always feels close, keeping you motivated to move forward.

Since energy levels vary, customize sprints to match your natural peaks. If mornings are your high-energy period, schedule Pomodoros then for tasks that demand focus, such as writing, problem-solving, or creative work. If you're sharpest in the evening, shift demanding work accordingly. Save administrative or routine tasks for low-energy times, such as after lunch or late in the afternoon, when focus tends to wane. For particularly creative projects, a 25-minute sprint may feel short—stretch it to 40 or 50 minutes if you're in a flow state, then take a break of longer than 5 minutes. Make the method fit your mind and body, rather than squeezing yourself into a rigid structure.

Timers are essential—not just for tracking time—but as a visual and auditory signal to focus or switch gears. Any basic timer will work, but apps can add helpful features. Focus Booster offers simple controls and automatically tracks your sprint history. TomatoTimer is a no-frills browser tool that won't distract you with extra features. Forest gamifies focus: stay on task and a digital tree grows; get distracted, and it withers. Whether you prefer a simple hourglass on your desk or a digital clock on your screen, having a visible timer anchors your intention and creates a physical reminder that it's work time.

Interruptions happen. Meetings, calls, or unexpected requests will occasionally break a sprint. Don't abandon the session. Pause the timer if possible and note where you left off—a sticky note does the trick. When you return, either finish the remaining time or restart the sprint if you've lost your groove. For big projects—writing a report, building a presentation—stack multiple Pomodoros with short breaks. But if your focus is fading, honor the pause; you'll likely return sharper after a quick rest.

Some days will spiral out of control no matter what. The aim isn't perfection, just progress. Even two focused sprints on a chaotic day are a win. On better days, six Pomodoros can dramatically boost your output without draining your energy. Each completed session adds up, and over time, you'll see that even a jumbled day can end with meaningful progress if you keep returning to these focused bursts.

Not all tasks require Pomodoros—deep creative work or batch tasks may not fit the cycle. Adapt the technique as needed: use Pomodoros to start hard tasks, chip away at massive projects, or power through routine chores stealing mental bandwidth. If you're on a team or working remotely, encourage everyone to share their focus times, and then schedule meetings around these periods to minimize interruptions and maximize collective output.

Experiment with session durations and break types to match your workflow and body clock. Try starting tomorrow with a single Pomodoro and see its effect. That timer might just become your push, not only to start but to keep coming back—even when distractions threaten to derail your best-laid plans (Lmay, n.d.).

INBOX ZERO FOR NON-STOP EMAILERS

Opening an inbox crowded with hundreds or thousands of unread messages creates a unique kind of dread. That alarming red badge, the endless bolded messages, and every "quick question" email all stack up —not just as digital clutter but as emotional baggage. A messy inbox is a daily, nagging reminder of unfinished business, fueling anxiety and procrastination. Promises to "handle it later" rarely dent the pile; it keeps growing unless tackled head-on.

Not just for productivity enthusiasts, Inbox Zero is a practical solution for anyone overwhelmed by the relentless demands of digital life. The goal? End each day (or at least each week) with an empty inbox. This doesn't mean instant replies to everything. Instead, each message is answered, filed, or deleted quickly. Clearing the backlog removes stress, breaks the cycle of avoidance, and eliminates the fear of losing important messages beneath a mountain of unread notifications.

Resetting Your Inbox

Inbox Zero is a process, not magic. Start with a clean-up session: block off 60–90 minutes, free from distractions, and begin triaging. Delete or archive anything unnecessary—old newsletters, expired promos, outdated invites—without hesitation. Then, batch process: group similar emails (all scheduling, all approvals, all questions) and handle them together. This reduces mental fatigue from switching between unrelated topics. For emails requiring follow-up, use organizational folders. Move them to "Action" for this week's tasks, "Waiting" for those pending responses, or "Archive" for completed items you might need later.

Using Filters, Folders, and Unsubscribing

Filters and folders are invaluable tools. Automate sorting so receipts, newsletters, and automated notifications bypass your main inbox and settle into dedicated folders. This instantly reduces distraction without manual work. If your inbox is cluttered with subscriptions or sales emails, go on an unsubscribe spree: click the unsubscribe link in every promo, without compromise. If you're unsure about deleting, collect questionable senders in an "Unsubscribe Review" folder and revisit it in a month—you'll likely find you don't miss most of them.

Maintaining Inbox Zero

Staying at Inbox Zero isn't about heroic weekend email marathons; it's about building simple daily habits that keep the mess from piling up in the first place. The "2-minute reply rule" is your secret weapon: if you can knock out a response in under two minutes, just do it right then (Clear, n.d.). For anything longer, resist the urge to dive in immediately. Instead, set specific email check-in times—maybe 10 a.m., 2 p.m., and right before you wrap up for the day.

Here's the key: keep your email closed outside those windows and silence those notifications. I know it feels scary at first, but constant pings are productivity killers that leave you exhausted for no good reason. Every Friday, take ten minutes for cleanup: archive stale items, clear your "Action" folder, and check if those "Waiting" messages have finally received replies.

Automate and Delegate

Boost efficiency with templates and automation. Build canned responses to routine questions ("What's your availability?" "Can you resend that file?"). For recurring requests, such as meetings, save a basic template ("I'm available [insert days/times]—let me know what works"). Auto-replies can set boundaries: "Thanks for your note! I check emails at 11 a.m. and 3 p.m. and will get back to you soon." This keeps expectations clear and your inbox manageable.

If possible, delegate: set up rules to send certain emails straight to team folders or an assistant. In shared inboxes, use color-coding so priority messages stand out. Consider integrating your email with a digital task manager, immediately turning actionable emails into tasks with due dates helps prevent them from slipping through the cracks.

The Real Goal

Inbox Zero is not about perfection or responding obsessively. Its true purpose is reclaiming peace of mind and mental clarity. With a clear inbox—even if not always literally empty—you stop worrying about hidden urgencies and focus on things that matter—instead of carrying that persistent, low-level anxiety in the background.

COMPREHENSIVE PRACTICAL IMPLEMENTATION GUIDES

You don't have to figure out these strategies on your own or struggle with vague instructions. I've created five practical implementation guides that take you step-by-step through each technique covered in this chapter. These aren't just theoretical overviews—they're detailed, practical resources designed to help you successfully implement each strategy in your real life, regardless of your experience level or work situation.

Each guide provides complete instructions for setup, daily use, troubleshooting common challenges, and customizing the approach to fit your unique circumstances. The Kanban board guide shows you exactly how to create your visual workflow system, whether you prefer digital tools like Trello and Notion or simple sticky notes on your wall. You'll learn how to structure your board, move tasks efficiently, and use visual progress tracking to maintain momentum even during busy periods.

The Time-Blocking guide transforms your chaotic schedule into protected blocks of focused time. You'll discover how to map your energy patterns to your most important tasks, create flexible blocks that withstand real-world interruptions, and build white space into your calendar for breathing room. The guide includes specific techniques for handling meeting overload, unexpected demands, and the challenges of working from home.

Task Batching eliminates the scattered feeling of constantly switching between different types of work. This guide teaches you how to group similar activities, create efficient batch processing sessions, and design themed days that work with your brain's natural focus patterns. You'll learn to batch everything from emails and phone calls to creative work and administrative tasks.

The Pomodoro Technique guide moves beyond the basic 25-minute timer to help you customize sprint lengths based on your energy levels, task complexity, and natural rhythms. You'll discover how to handle interruptions, adapt the technique for different types of work, and use it to build sustained focus, not rigid time management.

The Inbox Zero guide provides a systematic approach to email management that relieves the stress of an overflowing inbox. You'll learn the complete reset process, how to set up automation and filters, maintain daily habits that prevent email overwhelm, and integrate your email system with your broader productivity approach.

Getting started is simple—access all five guides through the exclusive resource hub using the link or QR code below.

Use the link here: https://bit.ly/MyAntiProcrastinationToolkit

Or use this QR code:

These guides work with whatever system you're already using—Google Calendar, Notion, pen and paper—so you won't need to overhaul everything. The goal isn't perfection but building sustainable habits that fit your real life. If you fall off track, the guides help you restart without guilt or complicated procedures.

Next, we'll explore how to maintain momentum when setbacks happen, making productivity a steady ally rather than a source of stress.

MAKE A DIFFERENCE WITH YOUR REVIEW

HELP SOMEONE BREAK FREE
FROM PROCRASTINATION

"The best way to find yourself is to lose yourself in the service of others."

MAHATMA GANDHI

You know what feels amazing? **Helping someone else get unstuck.** And right now, you have a chance to do exactly that.

Remember that feeling when you first realized procrastination wasn't your fault? When you discovered there were real, practical ways to break free from the cycle of delay and frustration? **Someone else is searching for that same breakthrough right now.**

My mission is to make overcoming procrastination simple and doable for everyone—no matter how busy life gets or how many times they've tried before.

But here's the thing: I can't reach everyone who needs this help. That's where you come in.

Most people choose books based on reviews. They want to know if something actually works before they invest their time and hope. So I'm asking you to **help a fellow procrastinator by leaving a quick review.**

It costs nothing and takes less than two minutes, but it could change someone's entire relationship with productivity. **Your honest review could help**...

- **one more parent finally tackle that project** they've been putting off for months.
- **one more professional stop feeling behind** and start feeling in control.
- **one more student break the cycle** of last-minute panic and all-nighters.
- **one more person stop beating themselves up** and start making real progress.
- **one more dream actually happen** instead of staying stuck in "someday" mode.

Think about it: **if this book is helping you even a little bit, imagine what your few words could mean to someone who's still struggling**. Someone just like you were before you started reading.

To make a difference, simply scan the QR code below and leave a review. Share what worked for you.

If you love helping others, you're my kind of person. Thank you from the bottom of my heart for paying it forward!

Bobby

CHAPTER 5
MASTERING MOTIVATION—HOW TO STAY DRIVEN WHEN YOU'D RATHER NOT

REWARD STACKING—TURNING SMALL WINS INTO BIG MOTIVATION

Have you ever noticed how checking even a small task off your list gives you a subtle thrill? Whether it's sending a tough email or submitting an expense report, that satisfaction isn't random—your brain is wired to crave rewards. While we admire lofty goals, it's those quick hits of progress that keep us moving, especially when motivation is low. Far from trivial, this process is biological and, when leveraged, can fuel your momentum.

Here's why: each time you finish a task and recognize it, your brain releases dopamine—the same 'feel-good chemical' from Chapter 1 that now works for you instead of against you. But dopamine isn't just about happiness; it boosts your drive and conditions your brain to seek out more of that rewarding feeling. When you tick boxes or move sticky notes to the "done" column, you're conditioning your brain to keep going. Studies show that immediate rewards—those given right after you complete something—supercharge this cycle, making you more likely to push through even boring or draining activities (Kelley, 2018). The closer the reward is to the effort, the more powerful the effect.

You can make this work for you through reward stacking—purposefully pairing each achievement, no matter how minor, with something you genuinely enjoy. This approach isn't about bribing yourself or feeling guilty about rewards. Instead, it's about making fulfillment part of your workflow, not just the final destination. Think of it as inserting little sparks of joy into your daily grind. For example, reserve your favorite podcast for when you're sorting receipts, or always follow up a tough report with a walk or a specialty coffee.

You don't need to reserve rewards for significant accomplishments. Long workdays rarely leave time for grand gestures, but even a five-minute break on social media after clearing your inbox can refresh your energy. Upgrading your workspace after a big project—maybe a new lamp or chair—turns progress into a tangible, lasting reward. These rewards don't have to cost much or take a long time; what matters is that they're meaningful to you and are linked to your effort, not just the outcome.

Laying out your reward stacks can transform those days when motivation is low. Writing them down helps prevent falling into old habits or forgetting to celebrate progress. Here's one way to do it: keep a list of tasks you usually avoid and, for each, jot down a reward that actually excites you. Some are instant (finish reviewing contracts, then take a Spotify break), while others are saved for bigger milestones (tie up this quarter's budget review, then treat yourself to takeout). The aim is to link each reward to a specific achievement.

Reward Stacking Worksheet: Link Your Effort to Enjoyment

Pick a task you dread or delay. Use these prompts to design your own mini reward stack:

- Task:

  ____

- What makes this task difficult for you? (e.g., boring, stressful):

  ____

- Quick reward after finishing (5–10 min):

  ____

- Bigger reward after finishing a set or project:

  ____

- How will you keep this reward feeling special and not just routine? (e.g., only allow yourself your favorite treat after this task): ____

Try applying this worksheet to three tasks this week. Maybe let yourself enjoy a comedy podcast while updating your résumé. Or reward a stretch goal at work with the new stationery you've wanted.

Here are quick reward ideas if you're stuck:

- Spend five guilt-free minutes on social media
- Stretch by an open window
- Enjoy a special coffee or tea
- Watch a saved YouTube video
- Order from a favorite restaurant for a big win
- Upgrade a desk accessory
- Take a ten-minute walk
- Text a friend to celebrate your win

Not everything good has to be earned, but pairing effort and enjoyment makes work less punishing and more fulfilling. The dopamine from those small achievements fuels your next step, especially when work feels overwhelming.

People who stick with their goals aren't relying on sheer willpower; they make progress feel rewarding as they go. You can create this drive by stacking fun rewards alongside your most important tasks. Let yourself celebrate every bit of progress, no matter how small. That's how momentum becomes routine, and motivation turns from luck into reliability.

IMPLEMENTATION INTENTIONS: IF-THEN PLANNING FOR FOLLOW-THROUGH

Ever find yourself swearing you'll start a task, only to freeze when the moment arrives? Motivation disappears, and you end up putting things off. You're not alone. Sometimes sheer intention just isn't enough. That's where implementation intentions come in. This is a science-backed strategy that takes the guesswork out of getting started. Instead of hoping you'll have the willpower when it counts, you create a clear mental shortcut: "If X happens, then I will do Y." It sounds simple, but it's a powerful way to bridge the gap between your intentions and your actions.

Researchers have shown that forming these if-then plans can almost double your chances of following through on challenging tasks (Wieber et al., 2015). Why does it work so well? Because your brain likes specifics. Broad goals like "I'll try to answer emails today" are easy to wiggle out of. But when you decide ahead of time what you'll do in a specific situation, your mind doesn't have to scramble for a response. The decision is already made. You're just following instructions you set for yourself earlier—no debate, no negotiation.

Let's break down how you can use this in your day-to-day life. Think about the moments that trip you up most often. Maybe it's that flood of emails you dread every morning, or the sense of overwhelm after a string of back-to-back meetings. Start by naming the trigger—what's the situation or feeling that usually leads to procrastination? Then pick a concrete action that you'll take when it happens. For example, "If I feel paralyzed when looking at my inbox, then I will process only the top five emails." Or "If I get stuck while planning a project, then I break it down into three micro-tasks I can do right away."

You can use implementation intentions for time-based triggers, too. "If it's 9 a.m., then I will open my project tracker and start my first Pomodoro sprint." "If I get interrupted by a colleague or a Slack ping, then I will jot down exactly where I stopped and set a five-minute timer to return to that spot." These little scripts act as tripwires for your habits—they kick in when your brain starts looking for an escape route.

Embedding if-then scripts into your routine doesn't require extra tools or fancy apps. All you need is a notepad or your favorite digital list. Try writing down three if-then plans tonight for tomorrow's biggest challenges. Here are some templates to get you started:

- "If my phone buzzes during deep work, then I'll silence it for 30 minutes."
- "If I start to feel bored during a routine report, then I'll play instrumental music until it's done."
- "If it's noon and I haven't moved in hours, then I'll walk around the block or do some stretches."
- "If I finish my first meeting, then I'll review my top priority before checking messages."

Having these scripts ready helps you to act instead of react. They're like mental shortcuts that cut through hesitation and doubt. You can also build them into shared routines with teammates or accountability buddies: if our meeting runs long, then we'll spend the last two minutes choosing one action item to work on before logging off.

Many professionals use this approach every day without even realizing it. Picture a remote worker who constantly gets hit with surprise Zoom calls. She sets her own rules. If an unexpected meeting pops up, then she'll immediately block ten minutes afterward for solo catch-up work—no emails or pings allowed. When distractions threaten to derail her focus, she returns to her if-then plan and avoids slipping into frustration or avoidance.

Or imagine a manager who often loses steam after lunch. He writes, "If I feel sluggish at 1 p.m., then I will spend ten minutes outlining tomorrow's tasks." Instead of scrolling through his phone or wandering through the office kitchen, he uses an if-then plan to steer himself gently back on course.

Try this exercise yourself: list two daily triggers that make you procrastinate—maybe it's fatigue at 3 p.m., or stress after opening your inbox. Next to each one, write a simple action that feels easy and specific. Keep these scripts visible—sticky notes on your screen, reminders in your calendar, or even a checklist on paper.

It doesn't have to be complicated or formal. The more you practice, the more automatic these responses become. Over time, your brain links each trigger to an action like muscle memory—no deliberation required. You're quietly building a buffer against those old patterns that used to slow you down.

With if-then planning, you're not relying on heroic bursts of motivation or hoping tomorrow will be different. You're giving yourself practical tools that make showing up easier, even on tough days or during chaotic weeks. Every script you put in place is one less decision weighing on your mind and one more step toward consistent action, no matter what comes up next.

THE POWER OF TINY CELEBRATIONS

It's wild how a tiny celebration can lighten your mood and recharge your motivation, even in the middle of a busy workday. The first time I tried it, I felt a little goofy. I had just sent out a big, overdue proposal and, instead of barreling ahead to the next thing, I paused for a quick fist pump. That tiny burst of energy shifted my entire afternoon. There's science behind this, too. Habit experts like BJ Fogg have shown that micro-celebrations reinforce habits in your brain. Every time you mark a win, even a small one, you're strengthening the neural pathways that make a connection between getting something done and a sense of achievement, which makes it easier for the brain to repeat the successful action (Fogg, 2024). The real secret isn't in the size of the achievement; it's in the emotional payoff you create for yourself on the spot.

You don't need a confetti cannon or an elaborate reward to celebrate. In fact, the best micro-celebrations are simple, spontaneous, and personal. Maybe you do a little victory dance, even if it's just a subtle shoulder shimmy, after ticking off a stubborn task—yes, right at your desk. Perhaps you whisper "nailed it" under your breath after finishing a tough call. Some people keep a tiny bell or chime on their desk and ring it when they hit their top priority for the day. That sound becomes the signal that something good just happened, and over time, your brain starts to crave that moment. I've heard from folks who high-five themselves in the mirror after sending an email they've been putting off. It sounds silly until you try it and notice how your energy shifts.

Another creative way to keep the celebration going is by sharing your wins with others. Posting your "win of the day" in a digital community or accountability group can multiply the impact. You get a double dose of good vibes—once from recognizing your progress, and again from getting support or virtual applause from people who get it. If you're working remotely or feel isolated at work, this can be a game-changer. I've seen teams start Slack threads for daily victories, where someone will cheerfully announce, "Wrapped up that gnarly report!" and others jump in with emojis or GIFs in response. That collective energy makes even solo work feel communal.

The real magic happens when you make celebration a habit, not just an occasional treat. Try keeping a "celebration log," a running list in Notion, Google Docs, or even an old-school journal. Jot down what you accomplished and how you marked the moment. Over time, you'll see patterns—which types of wins make you happiest, which celebrations give you the biggest boost, and how your mood shifts on days you skip this ritual. You're not competing in a productivity contest— you're building emotional awareness and tracking what actually works for you. Some people notice that their best days aren't the ones with the most tasks finished, but those days when they truly celebrated each win along the way.

Personalizing your celebrations is key. If victory dances aren't your thing, maybe you treat yourself to a slow stretch at your desk, or light a candle before moving on to the next project. For some folks, it's as simple as taking three deep breaths with their eyes closed after conquering a challenging task. Others snap a quick photo of their tidy workspace or of the empty coffee mug that means another report is done. The point isn't what you do—it's that you pause long enough to let yourself feel proud and energized by progress.

I've had clients who completely transformed their workdays by leaning into these tiny celebrations. One marketing specialist I worked with used to dread her Monday mornings: emails piling up, back-to-back meetings, motivation tanking by noon. She started ringing a bell every time she sent out her top-priority email for the day. At first, it felt awkward, but soon her coworkers noticed and started cheering along from across the open office. What began as a solo ritual became a team moment that cut through Monday blues and made tough starts feel lighter.

Others have found energy in even quieter ways. A project manager told me she rewards herself with five minutes of music and chair dancing after wrapping up each client call—no skipped steps allowed. Another remote worker uses colored sticky notes and adds a bright star sticker every time she completes something she's been avoiding. By Friday, her monitor is covered in stars, and she feels like she's won something real.

If you want to test the emotional impact for yourself, try this exercise: at the end of each workday this week, write down one thing you're proud of—big or small—and one way you celebrated it. It could be as tiny as standing up and stretching or as bold as sharing your win with a friend over text. Notice how your energy carries into the next task or even the next morning. You'll probably find that these micro-celebrations don't just make work more fun—they make starting again tomorrow feel just a little bit easier.

Tiny celebrations aren't about being childish or distracting yourself from serious work—they're about teaching your brain to associate effort with joy instead of dread. When progress feels good, you naturally want more of it. That's motivation you can count on, even when everything else feels tough.

MAKING BORING TASKS SATISFYING (GAMIFICATION & HABIT HACKS)

Some workdays, it feels like your to-do list is a string of chores nobody really wants to do: expense reports, inbox cleanout, calendar updates. Those tiny admin tasks keep piling up. It's easy for these jobs to drain your energy, especially if you're not seeing any real payoff. But what if you could flip the script and make even the dullest routines more engaging? That's where gamification steps in. Imagine treating your daily grind like a game, not a slog. Turning tasks into playful challenges taps into the same motivations that get people hooked on video games: points, levels, streaks, and the thrill of beating your own record. The aim is to make work feel just a little more interesting—enough that your brain wants to keep playing—without just pretending it's fun. Research shows that adding elements like points or streaks can increase motivation by giving your brain a clear goal and instant feedback (Abdaal, 2024). When you track progress visually or compete with yourself or others, you create a loop that keeps you coming back for more.

You can start simple. Use a habit app on your phone—something like Habitica or Streaks—which are explored in greater detail in Chapter 7, and transform everyday routines into quests with rewards, badges, and leaderboards. Suddenly, checking off "send invoices" or "clear Slack messages" isn't just another box to tick; it's progress toward a new badge or keeping a streak alive. The more days you log in and complete your mini missions, the higher your score and the longer your streak. It's a small trick, but it works because it gives structure and feedback where there usually isn't any. Some people love setting a personal record—maybe you time yourself on how fast you can finish your weekly timesheet or see if you can shave off a minute from last week's performance. Others take things up a notch by bringing in friendly competition—challenge a coworker to see who clears their inbox first or who completes more recurring tasks in a week. Even the smallest contest can inject just enough excitement to get you moving.

Gamification doesn't have to be high-tech or complicated. You can build playful challenges into your day using pen and paper. Make a bingo card of your least favorite chores, and mark off boxes until you hit "bingo." Or sketch out a "level up" tracker on a sticky note—each completed round of admin work moves you up a level. After five levels, you reward yourself with something special (maybe new pens or lunch from your favorite spot). Some folks create DIY leaderboards and update them at the end of every week, tracking how many days they hit their top three priorities.

Habit hacks can also take the edge off boring routines. Pair something dull with something you already enjoy—a classic approach called temptation bundling. For instance, save your best playlists for when you're sorting receipts or reserve that true-crime podcast only for laundry folding. Your brain starts to associate the task with pleasure, making it much less of a chore to get started. If music isn't your thing, maybe it's lighting a candle or using a scented hand lotion every time you tackle invoices or budget spreadsheets. These sensory cues help anchor habits by giving your brain something pleasant to look forward to.

Theme days are another secret weapon. Instead of randomly sprinkling admin work or personal finance tasks throughout the week, give each day a theme: "Admin Tuesday," "Finance Friday," "Wellness Wednesday." Clustering similar jobs together reduces decision fatigue and helps you slip into the right headspace faster. When you know Tuesday afternoons are always for paperwork, there's less mental resistance, and it becomes easier to get into the groove and finish more in one go.

If you want to really dial in your own gamified system, take ten minutes now for this challenge worksheet:

Build Your Personal Productivity Game

- What are your top three most boring recurring tasks? List them.
- What game element would make each one less tedious? (Points, streaks, time trials, badges)
- Which app or tool appeals to you? (Habitica, Streaks, old-school paper chart)

- What's one way to add friendly competition? (Colleague challenge, accountability buddy)
- What habit hack makes the task easier? (Music pairing, podcast, theme day)
- How will you track progress and celebrate "leveling up"?

Fill this out for one task today—maybe start with the thing you avoid most. Give yourself permission to experiment and tweak as needed until something clicks.

When you infuse your routines with game-like elements and habit hacks, you shift the focus from dread to curiosity. You stop asking, "How fast can I get this over with?" and start wondering, "How can I make this better—or even fun—this time?" That little bit of playfulness is sometimes all it takes to turn chores into mini victories that feel good. Work doesn't have to be fun all the time, but it shouldn't always feel like punishment either. Making things playful is about working with your mind instead of against it, letting progress become its own reward.

THE SCIENCE OF "WHY"—CONNECTING TASKS TO YOUR DEEPER VALUES

Most days, it's tempting to believe that motivation is just about energy or mood. But if you peel back the surface, there's often something bigger beneath your resistance or drive—a connection to what truly matters to you. The science is pretty clear: when you see a link between the stuff you do and your deeper hopes or values, motivation becomes steadier and less fragile. You're not just chasing a deadline or a pat on the back; you're feeding something that has meaning. Think about the last time you powered through a long, dull spreadsheet because you knew it would clear your evening for family dinner, or when you stayed late to prep slides that supported a cause or vision you care about. In those moments, the work felt different. It wasn't just another box to check—it was a step toward something bigger.

I see this all the time among professionals who manage to stay focused even when the work itself isn't glamorous. Take someone who works in finance but is passionate about animal rescue. Filing expense reports isn't thrilling but reframing it as "keeping my finances in order so I have more time and stability to volunteer on weekends" shifts the energy entirely. Suddenly, routine tasks aren't just chores; they're acts of service that honor your values. The same goes for the parent who slogs through confusing HR forms after hours—not because they love paperwork, but because they want to be fully present at home without work stress bleeding into dinner time. When you know what matters most, it's easier to push through even when you'd rather not.

If you've never asked yourself what actually moves you, this is your invitation. Everyone's "why" looks different—maybe it's creativity, stability, freedom, community, or growth. Sometimes it's a mix of those things. When you pause and name your core values, you point yourself back to purpose when motivation gets shaky. You stop seeing tasks as isolated annoyances and start recognizing them as building blocks that create a bigger picture.

Here's a simple reflection exercise to help uncover your drivers:

Worksheet: Why This Task Matters to Me (and My Future)

1. Pick a task you've been avoiding.
2. Ask yourself: if I finished this, what would it make possible?
3. Who benefits from me doing this well? (Could be you, your family, your team, or even clients.)
4. What value does this connect to? (E.g., freedom, security, creativity, connection)
5. Write a one-sentence script reframing the task: "Completing [task] supports [value/outcome]."

For example:

- "Completing this monthly report gives me peace of mind and helps my team make better decisions."
- "Filing these expense reports keeps my finances clear so I can travel more without guilt."

- "Processing these emails today means I can leave work on time and be fully present for my kids."

These scripts aren't for show; they're reminders that help anchor your day-to-day grind in something lasting. They don't make boring work magically exciting, but they do remind you why it's worth showing up.

The real shift comes when you practice this reframing consistently. I've seen a project manager transform her relationship with admin routines by connecting them with reliability—she realized that handling all the small stuff made her the teammate everyone trusted when big projects landed. A developer told me he once hated debugging code until he reframed it as supporting his team's creative goals instead of just fixing mistakes. With this shift in mindset, tedious testing felt like collaboration instead of punishment.

One story stands out—a dad who struggled with procrastination on client reports for months. He always felt behind, which led to late nights and weekends spent catching up instead of being present with his family. After reflecting, he realized each report he finished early was a piece of his evening reclaimed for bedtime stories and movie nights. This didn't erase the stress of deadlines, but it gave him a reason to care about getting ahead rather than treading water during the week.

Try this out for yourself. Next time you face a task that feels pointless or draining, pause and ask what's really at stake if you get it done—or don't. Sometimes the answer will surprise you. You may realize there's a hidden value that can transform how you feel about the work in front of you.

Connecting daily actions to your deeper *why* won't solve every challenge. However, it will cushion you against burnout and help motivation last when surface-level rewards fade. When your tasks are rooted in purpose, even tough days start to feel like progress instead of punishment.

As we wrap up this chapter on motivation, keep in mind that willpower is only half the story. It's the meaning behind your work—

the quiet pull of your values—that keeps you coming back long after external rewards lose their shine. In the next chapter, we'll explore building routines that adapt to real life, helping you keep moving forward even when things get messy.

CHAPTER 6

DESIGNING ROUTINES THAT STICK—EVEN WHEN LIFE GETS MESSY

MODULAR MORNING RITUALS FOR NON-MORNING PEOPLE

If you've ever woken up late, groggy, and already feeling behind, you know how quickly chaos can hijack your day. Much of morning advice comes from people who thrive before sunrise, packing in meditation, journaling, and long runs before others wake. That's not reality for most. Maybe your mornings involve hitting snooze, stumbling to the kitchen, or juggling kids and emails before coffee. If you're not naturally a morning person—or never know what the day will bring—traditional routines can feel out of reach. What if your routine could flex with your mood, energy, and circumstances instead of working against them?

A "morning routine" doesn't have to start at dawn or follow someone else's script. You don't have to overhaul your life to feel more grounded. A good routine begins whenever you wake up and meets you where you are, even if that's rolling out of bed at 8:30 a.m. with a video meeting in fifteen minutes. The secret isn't waking earlier or doing more. It's about creating a set of modular options—building blocks you can mix and match—so your mornings support you no matter what life brings.

Modularity is your lifeline on unpredictable days. Instead of forcing a rigid checklist, you draw from a menu of mini-rituals, picking what fits your time, mood, and needs. Maybe you're rushed and have only three minutes. Perhaps you've got twenty minutes to spare. You choose what's needed and leave the rest—without guilt.

Picture three "buckets": a 3-minute option, a 10-minute option, and a 20-minute option. On chaotic days, maybe all you do is make your bed and stretch for a moment. On slower mornings, you might add a quick meditation, set an intention, or review your calendar over coffee. None of these rituals needs to be fancy—they just need to work for you.

Here's a menu of morning ritual components:

- **3-Minute Moves:** Stretch your back and shoulders, take ten deep breaths by the window, make your bed, or clear a mug from your desk.
- **1-Song Dance Break:** Play an energizing song and move, even if you feel silly.
- **Single Intention:** Write one word or phrase that captures what matters most today (focus, patience, courage, etc.).
- **Calendar Coffee:** Sip something warm while scanning your calendar, just to flag surprises or deadlines.
- **Gratitude Glance:** Note one thing you're grateful for—even if it's just fresh socks or a quiet moment.

When building your menu, choose things that give you energy or clarity, not stress. If yoga isn't your style, try stretching or simply standing tall for a minute. If journaling sounds tiring, try a quick spoken note to yourself.

You don't have to do it all every day. The power is in asking, "What do I need most right now?" Sometimes you'll crave movement; other times, quiet—or simply a slower start as you get dressed.

A "minimum viable" routine is about setting the bar low enough that even on hard days, you show up for yourself. For example: "If I have five minutes, I'll make my bed and take three deep breaths." On better days: "If I have fifteen minutes, I'll stretch, sip coffee while checking my calendar, and note one thing I look forward to."

A financial analyst, Carrie, follows a "micro-morning" routine. She stopped beating herself up for not journaling. Now she simply makes her bed, drinks water, and reviews her top priority in her phone notes. Some days that's all she fits in; other days, she adds in a quick yoga session or takes her coffee outside.

Build-Your-Own Modular Morning Menu (Interactive Exercise)

Write down three morning rituals for each time slot—3 minutes, 10 minutes, 20 minutes—mixing physical (stretching), mental (intention-setting), and practical (calendar check) activities. Keep this menu visible—on your fridge, bathroom mirror, or as a phone wallpaper. Each morning, pick what fits your mood and schedule. Even if you do just one thing, it counts as a win.

Routines that last are flexible enough for real-life circumstances: late nights, early meetings, sick kids, or plain exhaustion. What matters is consistency over perfection and permitting yourself to adapt instead of forcing a routine that doesn't fit (Michal, 2020).

THE "RESET BLOCK": BOUNCING BACK AFTER A BAD DAY

We all know those days when nothing goes as planned: an unexpected meeting, a frustrating Slack message, or a missed deadline can throw your whole day off. The urge to just give up, thinking, "I'll fix it tomorrow," is strong. I've done that too many times, letting a bad day bleed into the rest of the week. That's when I need a "reset block"—a brief, intentional break to help me regroup and get back on track, no matter how off course things feel.

A reset block isn't about denying what went wrong or forcing yourself to fake positivity. It's a deliberate pause to stop a single rough moment from spiraling into an entire lost day or week. You give yourself a buffer—a space between frustration and progress—so one misstep doesn't define your entire timeline. Best of all, you don't need a full hour—even five minutes can do the trick.

A reset block has three simple, targeted steps. First is the physical reset. When you're stressed, your body gets tense—your shoulders bunch up, your jaw clenches, and your lungs forget to breathe deeply. Shaking off this tension matters more than it seems. Take a short walk, step outside for some fresh air, do ten jumping jacks, or simply stand and stretch. This isn't about getting fit; it's just movement, reminding your brain you're not stuck. Even rolling your shoulders or stretching above your head helps break the tension.

Next is the mental reset. When your mind is cluttered, it's hard to focus —especially after setbacks. Spend one minute clearing away visible clutter from your desk: toss trash, close unnecessary browser tabs, stack wayward papers. Or, if digital mess is the problem, do a quick sweep of your inbox or desktop, archiving or moving anything irrelevant into a single "Later" folder. No deep cleaning needed—just enough space to breathe and focus on what matters now.

Finally comes the quick win. This is where momentum returns. Choose a micro-task—the bite-sized task management approach we explored in Chapter 3—something doable in five minutes or less that gives you an easy success. Maybe it's replying to an overdue email, updating a project status, or sending that one Slack message you keep putting off. Keep it so small that there's no resistance. Finishing even a tiny task gives your brain a dopamine boost, proving you can still get things done and flipping the switch from stuck to moving.

Self-compassion is a crucial piece of any reset block. If you find yourself thinking, "I blew it again" or "I'll never catch up," interrupt that loop with something kinder. Try telling yourself, "Today was hard, but I get a fresh start now," or ask, "What's the smallest thing I could do to feel back on track?" I sometimes write reminders like this on sticky notes and put them on my monitor. They remind me I can start over anytime—not just on a perfect new morning.

Examples in Action

A software engineer I know had a major demo fail—coding errors everywhere—in front of the entire team. He wanted to quit for the day, but instead, he spent five minutes outside breathing, cleared error logs off his desktop, and rewrote a single failing test for one small win. It didn't solve everything, but it allowed him to end his day with a sense of accomplishment, not defeat.

A project coordinator, overwhelmed after a surprise fire drill, closed her eyes for a minute to count ten deep breaths, filed some scattered papers, and tackled one flagged "urgent" email for her win. These small acts were enough to help her face her task list again without feeling buried.

Reset Block Reminders

If you're feeling guilty over missed deadlines or mistakes, remember that setbacks are not failures of character, just normal parts of real work. A reset block is your permission to start fresh without shame, at any time of day. You're not erasing the mistake; you're refusing to let it decide the rest of your day.

Try these mindset prompts when things go sideways:

- "That meeting was brutal, but I'm allowed to reset."
- "Missing this deadline stings; what's one step I can take right now?"
- "Even if today unraveled, I get to regroup."

Some days will go wrong—that's just life. But with the reset block, chaos doesn't have to derail you. Instead of waiting for a magical fix, you make small steps to get yourself back on track. Remember: progress isn't perfection—it's just giving yourself permission to begin again (Miss Unconventional, n.d.).

ANTI-OVERWHELM WEEKLY PLANNING (ACTION LADDERS & PRIORITY MAPS)

For many, Sunday nights or Monday mornings bring as much anxiety as anticipation, with the pressure to do everything: meet deadlines, attend meetings, care for family, and (maybe) find time for yourself. Overwhelm often starts before the week even begins, just from the sheer volume of demands. A weekly planning system designed for real life—one that breaks big projects into small, prioritized pieces—can be the difference between feeling buried and getting things done.

Weekly planning isn't about making a flawless schedule you'll never change. It's about clarity, control, and building momentum one step at a time. My method blends action laddering with visual priority maps to turn chaos into doable sequences, even when surprises hit.

Action laddering involves breaking down a big project into incremental steps, progressing from the easiest steps to the hardest. Start at the lowest rung—the most approachable task—and work upward. Each finished step builds momentum and makes the next less intimidating. For example, a daunting client proposal's top rung might be "Send completed deck," but the first rung could be "Open last week's feedback email" or "Write one slide headline." Big goals shrink into clear, achievable wins.

Next is the priority map—a visual way to keep your focus on what truly matters, not on whatever pops up first. Quadrant maps are especially effective, dividing tasks into: urgent/important, not urgent/important, urgent/not important, and neither. Color-coding adds another layer: red for "Must-Do," yellow for "Should-Do," blue for "Nice-to-Do." Laying your week out like this reveals what's truly fueling your stress (often too many reds). This reduces decision fatigue because you no longer have to guess what matters every morning.

As a weekly routine, every Sunday, I use a simple worksheet starting with, "List your three most important outcomes for the week." These are key results, not just chores, like "Finish draft proposal," "Book pediatrician appointment," or "Run two marketing tests." For each, I break down action ladders from easiest to hardest, then map them onto my quadrant chart and assign colors by urgency and impact.

Real-Life Application

A friend who juggles remote work, a baking side biz, and two school-age kids swears by this method. She picks her three weekly must-wins: "Prep client pitch," "Deliver two cake orders," "Plan Saturday family outing." For each task, she breaks it down into smaller parts. For example, for a client pitch: prepare call notes, send call reminders, then conduct the call. "Must-Do" items are red (like confirming cake pickups) and go on her calendar first. "Should-Do" tasks (yellow) are slotted around the edges, such as updating her website. Blue sticky notes ("Nice-to-Do") are for optional things like sorting photos. She posts the map on her fridge so everyone knows her focus.

This method works because it provides structure and flexibility. If an unexpected event interrupts your week—a client issue or a sick child—you can rearrange sticky notes or drag digital tasks without scrapping the entire plan. The action ladder provides a quick win even on tough days; you can always grab a low-rung step and move forward.

Weekly Outcomes Worksheet

1. **List Your Three Most Important Outcomes:**
   - Outcome 1: _______________________________
   - Outcome 2: _______________________________
   - Outcome 3: _______________________________
2. **Break Down Each Outcome into Action Ladders:**
   - Smallest Step: _______________________________
   - Next Step: _______________________________
   - Final Step: _______________________________
3. **Create Your Priority Map:**
   - Place each task in the correct quadrant (Urgent/Important, etc.)
   - Color-code by priority: Red (Must-Do), Yellow (Should-Do), Blue (Nice-to-Do)
4. **Schedule Must-Dos First:**
   - Monday: _______________________________
   - Tuesday: _______________________________
   - Wednesday: _______________________________
   - ...and so on

This process takes about fifteen minutes once you're used to it and saves hours of indecision. You'll stop wasting time on low-impact work just because it's easy to check off—the real energy goes to what matters (Sumrell, 2024).

Digital and Shared Use

This approach is adaptable—digital boards like Trello or Notion handle mapping and rearranging with ease, while sticky notes work well for analog users. Families can use shared maps to manage school events and deadlines, freelancers can mix side gigs with errands, and anyone can maintain balance without feeling pulled in two directions.

Visual, sequenced planning tames overwhelm. Each completed step reinforces progress and makes tasks feel manageable. Over time, you gain resilience, not just productivity, and can focus on steady progress over perfection.

BUILDING BUFFER ZONES AND "WHITE SPACE" INTO YOUR CALENDAR

I can't count the number of weeks I've packed my calendar so tight that one minor hiccup—a meeting that ran long, a last-minute request, a tech glitch—sent the whole day spinning. You probably know the feeling: you end one Zoom call, breathe for thirty seconds, and a new meeting dings. Maybe you run from project to project, grabbing snacks between calls, answering Slack from your phone in the hallway, all while mentally juggling your growing to-do list. Without breathing room, stress compounds. You fall behind, tasks spill over into evenings and weekends, and your mind starts looking for any excuse to escape. This is a perfect storm for procrastination. It's not laziness—it's your brain rebelling against relentless pressure.

Science and real-life prove it: building "white space"—the intentional gaps between commitments—creates room for creativity, focus, and recovery. Some of my most creative ideas have bubbled up not during meetings or in front of a screen, but in the fifteen-minute pause before lunch or on a walk after a tough call. Companies that experiment with meeting-free afternoons or buffer times see more innovation and less burnout. One productivity study found that knowledge workers who protected calendar white space reported feeling less overwhelmed and solved problems faster than those who never stopped moving.

It's easy to tell yourself you "don't have time" for breaks, but the truth is you don't have time not to take them. Over-scheduling leads to task overflow. When one thing runs late, everything after it falls apart. Energy tanks, errors creep in, and suddenly you're working twice as hard to keep up. Without buffers, even small surprises—an unscheduled check-in or an urgent email—can derail your whole day. You end up multitasking just to survive, which is a recipe for distraction and mistakes.

To change this, you need to start seeing buffer zones as non-negotiable, like seat belts or locking your front door. The first step is awareness. Pull up last week's calendar—digital or paper—and highlight every spot where meetings bumped up against each other or tasks ran late. Where did you feel most frazzled? Where did things spill over? That's where you need white space.

Now, look at the week ahead and add 15-minute buffers between meetings whenever possible. If you can't move the meetings themselves, block out time before and after on your calendar—label it "buffer," "prep," or even "do not book." Use these windows for a quick stretch, a bathroom break, jotting down action items, or just staring out the window to reset your mind. Protect these gaps fiercely. If someone tries to schedule over them, ask if it can wait or offer an alternative slot. It takes practice to defend your time, but every protected buffer pays off.

End-of-day wind-down blocks are equally important. Reserve 30 minutes at the close of your workday—not for more work, but for review and closure. Use it to tie up loose ends, update your to-do list, clear your desk, and mentally transition out of work mode. This habit helps prevent urgent emails from bleeding into dinner or late-night worry spirals.

Handling the unexpected is where white space proves its worth: meetings will run long, clients will call with urgent requests, and colleagues will demand your attention. When that happens, resist the urge to shove everything else aside or work late into the night. Instead, use a "parking lot" list—a running note on paper or in your phone—for overflow tasks that can wait until tomorrow or next week. This keeps your focus on what's urgent now without losing track of less pressing items.

Learning to say no—or at least "not now"—is vital for keeping white space intact. I've practiced scripts that go like this: "I'm at capacity today—could we move this to later in the week?" or "I want to give this my full attention; is Thursday a better time?" Most people respect directness when you're clear about your limits (and you'll respect yourself more, too).

If you use Google Calendar or Outlook, color-code your white space so it stands out: maybe blue for buffers, green for wind-downs. Some people prefer hand-drawn planners with blank time blocks—whatever makes the space visible and harder to ignore. When you see an open stretch on your calendar, let it remind you that rest is not wasted—it's productive and necessary.

On my own calendar, I've started including recurring half-hour blocks labeled "no meeting zone" in red and fifteen-minute buffers in yellow before every big call. Even if someone tries to book over them, I have a visual cue that this time matters. A friend uses a paper planner with literal blank lines between appointments; a simple trick that keeps her from stacking commitments too closely.

White space isn't wasted time; it's the oxygen that lets you do your best work without drowning in demands. It helps ideas surface when you least expect them and gives you room to handle life's constant curveballs without spiraling into frustration or delay (ZCal, 2024).

RESETTING ROUTINES AFTER TRAVEL, SICKNESS, OR SETBACKS

Disruptions are a fact of life. Maybe you've just wrapped up a week of business travel, spent days home sick in bed, or had to drop everything for a family emergency. When you finally come back to your usual routines, it's normal to feel completely out of sync. Productivity books often overlook this reality, but if you've ever opened your laptop after a long break and felt lost, you know the struggle. The mess isn't just on your desk or in your inbox—it's in your head too. There's frustration in seeing unfinished projects, missed messages, and a tidal wave of new demands. Instead of a fresh start, it can feel like you're underwater before you even begin.

It's easy to fall into self-criticism when routines collapse. Your mind tells you that you've failed or that everyone else handles chaos better. I want to say, as clearly as possible: this is normal. Setbacks—whether from travel, illness, or significant life changes—aren't failures; they're part of the rhythm of real life. Even the most organized people get knocked off track. What matters isn't avoiding disruptions (you can't), but how gently and intentionally you rebuild after them.

When you're ready to get back in, start with a three-step reboot protocol: review, prioritize, re-engage. The first step is review—take a clear-eyed look at what's unfinished but leave judgment out of it. Scan your inbox, open your project tracker, and look over your calendar. Notice what's still waiting for you, but don't beat yourself up for what you didn't accomplish. The point is to get reoriented, not to tally failures. If a task has been hanging over you for a while, just acknowledge it without assigning blame.

Next comes prioritization. Don't try to do it all on your first day back; that's a recipe for disaster and more overwhelm. Instead, pick just one or two priorities that truly move things forward or bring relief. Maybe it's replying to your manager's email about an ongoing project or confirming a meeting that got rescheduled while you were away. Resist the urge to clear every message or finish every task at once. Focus on what matters and let the rest wait.

The final step is to re-engage with a low-stakes win. This is where momentum begins to return. Choose something small and doable—perhaps something that follows the 2-Minute Rule from Chapter 3—an easy win that helps shake off inertia. Maybe it's sending a single catch-up note to your team or prepping your workspace for tomorrow. You might even start by unpacking your bag or resetting your calendar before diving into anything more complicated. The value of that first win is in proving to yourself that you can start again—it's not just another productivity point.

Compassion makes this process work. The voice in your head might say, "You're so behind," but the truth is, everyone faces setbacks and disruptions. Try these scripts when the guilt creeps in: "It's normal to feel behind after time away," or "A single step is enough for today."

Permit yourself to have a messy restart rather than forcing perfection. (Learn more about self-compassion practices in Chapter 8.)

I remember returning from a week-long conference with a mountain of notes, receipts, emails, and not a clue where to begin. Instead of tackling everything at once (which just leads to anxiety), I reviewed my inbox without judgment, flagged just two must-dos—a follow-up email and submitting my expense report—and then reorganized my desk for the next day. That small reset was enough to snap me out of avoidance mode.

For those working remotely or juggling parenting along with their job, the chaos multiplies after disruptions like travel or illness. One parent I know keeps a post-disruption checklist taped inside her cabinet door: "Unpack bags, check school messages, review work calendar, send one update to boss." She adds one easy win—a quick walk outside or tidying her desk—before worrying about anything significant. Frequent travelers might include things like "recharge devices" or "reschedule missed calls" on their list before even glancing at larger projects.

Post-Disruption Reset Checklist

- Unpack bags and put away travel (or sick day) clutter
- Review your calendar for urgent deadlines or meetings
- Scan emails or messages—flag only critical ones for response
- Choose one priority task for today (not ten)
- Plan one easy win (reply to a friendly email, tidy up workspace)
- Reconnect with a colleague or team member (quick check-in)
- Give yourself permission to defer non-essential tasks until tomorrow

If you're tempted to push yourself too hard to catch up quickly, remember that after a setback, consistency beats intensity every time. Reboots aren't about heroic recoveries but about steady progress and self-kindness.

As this chapter wraps up, remember: routines exist to help you through the chaos, not just during smooth weeks. Disruptions will happen—travel plans change, illness strikes, emergencies pop up—but each time you reset with intention and patience, you prove that productivity comes from starting over with compassion and trusting momentum to return, not from perfection or rigid discipline.

In the next chapter, we'll look at how accountability boosts follow-through and keeps progress alive even when motivation wavers or life throws curveballs your way.

CHAPTER 7

ACCOUNTABILITY THAT DOESN'T RELY ON WILLPOWER

FINDING AND USING AN ACCOUNTABILITY BUDDY

Picture this: it's a regular workday, and you're stuck procrastinating on an important task. You know it's essential and time-sensitive, but motivation is nowhere in sight. Suddenly, your phone buzzes—a message from someone who genuinely understands this struggle. She's checking in, asking, "Did you eat your frog today?" Instantly, you feel a bit more motivated. That's the simple magic of an accountability buddy.

Having someone in your corner completely changes how you approach your to-dos. An accountability buddy is a partner, not a critic. They check in with you, share their progress, and ask about yours. The dynamics shift from "I have to do this alone" to "We're in this together." Mutual support replaces pressure. You'll celebrate wins, talk through setbacks, and never worry about embarrassment. For many professionals, solo attempts often fail because it's easy to ignore your own goals, but it's much harder to brush off a friend who genuinely cares. Peer support taps into our drive for connection while building in accountability. Research shows that sharing your intentions increases your chances of success, and having weekly check-ins can boost follow-through up to 95% (Chaudhuri, 2023).

Choosing the right accountability partner matters. Don't just default to your closest friend or coworker—look for someone with similar ambitions or struggles, even if your goals differ. What matters most is a shared focus on progress and the ability to laugh at setbacks. Make sure your communication styles match—if you dislike phone calls, partner with someone who prefers texts. Think about check-in frequency; daily prompts work for some, while others prefer weekly wrap-ups. Time zones and schedules also matter; if you're both busy or working remotely, asynchronous updates like voice notes or scheduled messages can be practical.

The best accountability partnerships have structure without being rigid. Set expectations together. How often will you check in? What qualifies as a win? Are you focusing on one big goal or several small ones? Don't overcomplicate it—focus on simple wins. Try a "quick win" and "stuck point" format: each shares one thing achieved since the last check-in and one struggle. Swap encouragement, brainstorm solutions briefly if needed, and keep weekly calls concise—fifteen minutes is usually enough. If live calls don't work, agree to send texts, voice memos, or GIFs at set times.

A typical check-in might go:

- "What was your biggest quick win since last time?"
- "Where did you get stuck?"
- "What will you focus on before our next check-in?"
- "How can I support you this week?"

Stay honest and friendly. If someone falls off track, avoid blame; instead, discuss what got in the way and adjust together.

Consider these real-life examples. Two remote workers, one in Boston and one in Denver, texted each morning about their main tasks and checked in at night with a simple response. Within a few months, they found themselves completing demanding tasks earlier and feeling less anxious about work. In another case, two friends at different jobs held a ten-minute video call every Friday around noon. They each shared one win and one challenge—sometimes work-related, sometimes personal. The brief calls kept them accountable without overwhelming their schedules, and both felt more energized seeing a fellow professional face similar issues.

Interactive Element: Accountability Buddy Quick Start Guide

Take five minutes to jot down:

1. What's one recurring task or project you struggle to finish solo?
2. Who in your network would make a good accountability buddy? Consider shared challenges, clear communication, and flexibility.
3. What check-in style works for you: text, call, video, or voice note? How often?
4. Send a quick message inviting that person to try a one-week accountability experiment.

Sample script: "Hey! I'm working on being more consistent with [your goal]. Want to try being accountability buddies for a week? Just quick check-ins, nothing serious. It could be helpful and even a little fun for both of us."

The best accountability partnerships are built on honest, low-pressure support. Updates should be brief, judgment-free, and focused on showing up. Progress counts even when it's imperfect or slow. You're creating a system where consistent effort is the goal, not perfection.

SELF-CONTRACTS AND PUBLIC COMMITMENTS

Writing a promise to yourself shifts a vague intention into a clear commitment. This isn't just ritual; it has real psychological weight. When you write out a goal, a deadline, and your name, you move your focus from daydreaming to action. What was once just in your head becomes physical and visible, looking back at you from a notebook, fridge, or phone screen. This is the essence of a self-contract—a written promise to do something specific by a certain time, often with stated steps and even consequences if you don't follow through. It might sound formal or awkward, but it works by giving you structure and clarity. It's not just a fleeting thought; it's a dividing line between "maybe" and "definitely."

To start, just grab any writing surface—a notebook, a scrap of paper, your phone's notes app. Write exactly what you want to accomplish and a real deadline, like: "I'll finish and submit my expense report by Thursday at 3 p.m." Be as specific as possible to avoid giving yourself loopholes. Next, add a consequence or contingency plan. This isn't about harsh punishment—it's about making the commitment tangible. You might promise, "If I don't submit by then, I'll update my manager explaining why," or "If I miss it, I owe myself an hour of work on Saturday morning." The idea is to create gentle accountability that keeps you on track without making you dread mistakes.

There's power in seeing your intention written out. You could write, "I will submit my proposal by Friday at noon. If I don't, I'll donate $20 to a coworker's charity." With skin in the game, urgency and responsibility increase. You can make it more tangible by signing, dating, and posting the note somewhere visible, such as your desk, laptop, fridge, or phone background.

But sometimes, even the most substantial written promise isn't enough. When motivation disappears or old habits persist, public commitments help. Sharing your goals publicly with friends, colleagues, or online raises the stakes. Social accountability is powerful; most people want to follow through when others are aware, especially with people they respect (Yildiz, 2025).

Public commitments can take many forms. You might post weekly priorities on a Slack channel, share a goal in a group chat, or even announce deadlines on social media if that feels encouraging. Some set up "launch dates" and notify their team early—not just as a heads-up, but to lock in the commitment. Others email colleagues: "I'm finishing my presentation by Thursday morning—hold me to it!" Even a lunch conversation about your intentions can spark action.

Of course, not every public commitment leads to encouragement— sometimes it can backfire, especially with a critical audience. Pick your audience carefully; choose supportive people or groups where there's more cheerleading than shaming, and where setbacks are met with empathy, not "told you so." If you don't have that at work, try a trusted friend or small group who understands your goals.

Before going public, pause and consider how you'd feel if you fell short. If it would motivate you and bring helpful support, proceed. If it would make you anxious or tempted to hide, consider dialing it back —share with a smaller or more private audience. The right amount of visibility pushes you forward without making you dread failure.

If you're new to public commitments, start small: share one weekly goal with a friend or coworker, and check in at the end of the week. Or post a single intention in a private group each Monday and report progress on Friday—no judgment, just honest check-ins.

Simply knowing someone else is aware often tips you from just planning to doing. Self-contracts and public commitments aren't miracles, but they're practical tools that help keep you honest and focused. When motivation fades, they make your promises feel real enough to act on—not just empty wishes floating in your head.

DIGITAL PROGRESS TRACKERS AND HABIT APPS THAT ACTUALLY WORK

If you love the feeling of ticking off a task, you're not alone. That little jolt of satisfaction from seeing progress—even in small doses—can drive real momentum. Digital progress trackers and habit apps can turn this feeling into daily action. However, not all of them fit seamlessly into every lifestyle. The key is finding a tool that matches your personality: a system simple enough to use with minimal effort yet motivating enough that you want to keep coming back.

As we saw in Chapter 5, there are plenty of apps out there, each with its own style. If you like simplicity, Streaks is a standout. It lets you track up to twelve habits, and the goal is to keep your streak alive. Just check off each task, and the app visually celebrates your progress—no distractions or unnecessary clutter. If you need more engagement, Habitica turns habits into a game. You earn points and rewards, build a character, and can join group quests. Skip a day, and your avatar weakens. Its playful, RPG (role-playing) approach can make chores fun and is perfect for anyone who enjoys a bit of competition or humor.

Other options worth considering include Done, which focuses on tracking how often you complete habits using simple graphs and colors, and Coach.me, which offers both free tracking and the chance to hire real coaches for support. Coach.me's intuitive design makes it easy to log achievements or set reminders with just a few taps. None of these require tedious setup—just enter your habits or goals, set reminders, and choose how frequently you want to check in, whether that's daily, weekly, or only on certain days.

These trackers are meant to make your progress visible without taking over your life. Start by listing three to five daily goals, like "start work by 9," "drink water," or "read for 10 minutes." Open your chosen app and enter each habit, assigning colors or icons if you want. For weekly goals, set up repeating check-ins or use dashboards with simple labels: green for done, yellow for in progress, red for needs attention. Apps like Habitica and Coach.me even allow you to add notes at each check-in, letting you track not just completion, but patterns or obstacles.

Making these trackers a natural part of your routine keeps them effective but requires little effort. Sync with your calendar so habits appear alongside meetings or use phone widgets for quick check-ins. Streaks and Done both offer Apple Watch and home screen widgets. For automation fans, tools like Zapier or IFTTT can log your day's progress into a spreadsheet, send you weekly summaries, or trigger congratulations for hitting a milestone—all without extra work.

One project manager uses her app for a quick review every Friday. She checks her color-coded dashboard—green means goal met, yellow means progress—and sometimes she adds a quick note about any obstacles that popped up. Her Friday check-in is as routine as checking email, giving her a chance to reset for the new week.

Motivation looks different for everyone. Some enjoy leveling up and earning badges, while others just want the satisfaction of a neat checklist. If you find yourself abandoning apps after a few days, consider why—was it too complicated, boring, or did it lack feedback? Experiment until you find something that clicks. The best tracker is the one you actually use: it nudges you when motivation fades but doesn't make you feel like you've failed if you miss a day.

If you're ready to try, download just one app: Streaks for simplicity, Habitica for fun, Done for visuals, or Coach.me for versatility. Enter a single habit that would make tomorrow easier if it became automatic. Add a reminder for the time you're most likely to act on it. Open the app once a day, check off your progress—don't worry about being perfect. Watch your small wins add up on your screen and in your everyday life (Zapier, 2024).

BUILDING YOUR OWN "STAND-UP" CHECK-IN ROUTINE

You've probably heard about stand-up meetings in tech or agile teams. There's something refreshing about the idea: a short, focused huddle where everyone lays out what they did, what they plan to do, and what's blocking their way. What most people don't realize is how well this routine works for solo professionals and small groups, not just big corporate teams. The beauty of a stand-up is its brevity and directness. In 5 to 10 minutes, you cut through noise, surface your intentions, and face your obstacles head-on. And trust me, you don't need a team of engineers or a fancy office to make this work. It's just about creating a daily rhythm that keeps you honest with yourself.

For individuals, the structure is so simple it's almost impossible to mess up: "Yesterday I..." "Today I will..." What's getting in my way? Each section prompts you to acknowledge progress, prioritize your next step, and name any blockers—big or small. The first time I tried this, I felt a little awkward, talking to myself out loud in my kitchen. But that awkwardness faded quickly as I realized how much lighter my head felt—no more vague, nagging sense of "I should do something." Each morning, I'd jot down three quick bullets: I finished the client report; I'll send it out today and schedule next week's meeting; my only blocker is waiting for feedback from Sarah. Some days, the blocker was just my own resistance to getting started. Naming it made it easier to tackle.

If you're working remotely or alone most of the time, keeping this routine digital makes sense. Open your favorite notes app, create a new page for each day, and fill out those three prompts. Or, if you prefer more accountability, create a daily check-in thread in your team's Slack or WhatsApp group—even if you're the only one posting at first. These micro-journals become a running log of your intentions and progress. They also help you spot patterns: maybe you notice every Wednesday, meetings wreck your focus, or specific projects always bring up resistance.

Groups can adapt the same structure with very little friction. A small team or friend circle might kick off the day with a quick round-robin on Zoom or Google Meet. The trick is to keep it tight: each person gets sixty seconds for their update. No rambling stories or derailed discussions—just a laser focus on what's moving forward and what's in the way. For remote teams spread across time zones, asynchronous check-ins are gold. Set up a shared Notion page or Google Doc where everyone drops their update before noon. You can read through your colleagues' notes when you log on, get a sense of momentum, and reach out if someone's stuck on something you can help with.

What makes these stand-ups stick isn't just habit—it's the psychological effect of putting your intentions into words where others might see them. Even if nobody responds every single day, the possibility creates just enough of a social nudge to make you want to show up and be consistent. No one wants to be the person who disappears for days or keeps saying "nothing to report." There's subtle peer pressure in a good way.

I know a freelancer who started her mornings by recording a voice memo on her phone—just a one-minute memo tops—where she answered those three prompts to herself. She kept them in a folder she could revisit whenever she felt lost midweek. Over time, she realized her blockers were almost always about vague next steps, not lack of motivation or skill. She started planning her day around making those next steps crystal clear.

There's also the story of three friends who started a weekly "Friday Wins" video call during the pandemic. Each person talked about their best accomplishment of the week, what they wanted to do next week, and what got in their way this time around—no judgment, no competition—just honest check-ins and a little bit of celebration. The calls quickly became something they looked forward to all week. The act of voicing their wins—no matter how small—gave everyone a boost going into the weekend.

If you want to experiment with this structure for yourself or your group, here's one way to get started: pick a time that's easy to remember—maybe right after you open your laptop or while you sip your first cup of coffee. Write down or say out loud these three prompts: "Yesterday I..." "Today I will..." What's getting in my way? If you're flying solo, keep a digital or paper log. If you're part of a team or group chat, post your answers there. At the end of the week, look back—not just at what you finished but at how your blockers shifted (or didn't). You might realize Mondays always trip you up because of meetings, or you do your best work after lunch.

These stand-up routines aren't about micromanaging yourself or others. They're a tool for building gentle momentum and clarity each day—like giving your brain a morning reset button. When the days blur together or motivation runs thin, this kind of routine gives you a small anchor. It's simple but powerful: state your intentions out loud, acknowledge what's holding you back, and move forward with purpose.

JOINING (OR CREATING) PROGRESS COMMUNITIES FOR PEER SUPPORT

Overcoming procrastination is far easier with support. The right progress community transforms lonely effort into lively, shared encouragement. Unlike passive chat groups, real progress communities thrive on regular check-ins, shared accountability, and honest conversations about wins and setbacks. Members value participation over perfection, cheer each other on, and lift each other up when motivation dips.

Finding the right group starts with platforms you already use. Facebook hosts productivity-focused groups like "Accountability for Ambitious Women" or "Daily Focus Sprints." Reddit's r/productivity has daily check-ins and sometimes even local meetups. Discord servers offer coworking rooms and community challenges in real time. Don't ignore local options—Meetup.com and Eventbrite list in-person accountability circles and coworking mornings. Read group descriptions and forums to find active, engaged communities with clear guidelines and real interaction.

If you can't find the right community, it's surprisingly easy—and often fun—to create your own. You don't need a big group; limiting it to three to five people ensures everyone contributes and gets noticed. Reach out to friends, coworkers, or acquaintances interested in getting more done or breaking out of procrastination. Suggest a low-pressure setup: maybe a private Slack or WhatsApp group, or a recurring Zoom call. Emphasize the informal, supportive nature—just check-ins and real talk, no lectures or pressure to be perfect.

The real value of a group comes from simple structure and consistent rituals. Clear ground rules are vital: keep feedback positive, maintain confidentiality, and avoid shaming anyone for missing a goal. Work together to decide on a check-in frequency, such as "Monday Goals," "Wednesday Reset," and "Friday Reflections," to plan the week and reflect on progress. Many groups add coworking rituals, like virtual pomodoro sprints, where members work together in silence, then briefly share completed tasks.

Celebrating success matters, but normalizing setbacks is just as vital. Some groups kick off Friday check-ins by asking, "What worked? What flopped? What did you learn?" This openness normalizes both wins and misses—whether landing a client or dropping the ball on tasks—reminding everyone that nobody has it all together. When someone stumbles, the group offers practical help or simple encouragement, which quickly restores motivation and keeps members coming back.

A couple of quick examples: Mia, a marketing consultant working from home, joined a Discord coworking group. Daily focus sessions and friendly support helped her feel less isolated and boosted her productivity. Darren, a remote-working dad, started a neighborhood group with two other parents. They'd swap weekly goals and advice over Zoom, helping each other stay organized while making parenthood feel less overwhelming.

Such communities aren't instant solutions, but they make it easier to form better habits and break out of isolation. Seeing others push through resistance inspires commitment, and everyone's shared drive makes routines feel more like belonging than burden (Wilde, 2023).

Remember: accountability thrives on connection, not pressure. Whether you join an existing community or start your own, the goal is finding people who genuinely understand the struggle. Progress feels more natural and setbacks become easier to recover from when you're not going it alone. Next, we'll explore what to do when old habits return—and how to bounce back with your momentum and confidence intact.

CHAPTER 8
WHEN RELAPSE HAPPENS—RELAPSE-RESCUE PROTOCOLS

UNDERSTANDING THE RELAPSE CYCLE—WHY OLD HABITS RETURN

Ever notice how one minute you're crushing your goals, knocking out work, maybe even feeling invincible, and the next, you wake up and realize you haven't touched your most important project in days? You wonder, "How did I end up back here?" This isn't just you. Relapses sneak in on everyone—even those LinkedIn productivity machines who seem unstoppable. The truth is, slipping back into old habits is not a sign you're doomed. It's an entirely normal part of building new routines. Your brain isn't betraying you—it's just following its wiring, especially when life gets bumpy.

Let's break down what's really going on behind the scenes. When you try to change how you work or live, you're forcing your brain to build new neural pathways. This takes energy and repeated effort. Your old habits are deeply carved neural pathways, strengthened by years of repetition. Think of them as well-worn shortcuts your brain has memorized and can follow without effort. When stress ramps up, deadlines explode, or you're running on empty after a rough week, your brain defaults to the familiar. In neuroscience, this fallback is about energy conservation: the brain chooses the easiest route when under pressure.

So, if procrastination or avoidance used to be your autopilot, it'll come roaring back when things get tough (Wood et al., 2023).

Relapse isn't just random—it's predictable. Certain triggers almost always set it off. For a lot of people, stress at work is high on the list. Maybe your inbox explodes with urgent requests, or your boss drops a last-minute project on your plate. Family demands can do it too: a sick child, a parent who needs help, or your own health taking a nosedive. Fatigue is another big one. After you've pushed hard for weeks— maybe finishing a product launch or closing out a big quarter—the letdown can leave you without mental fuel to keep up good habits. Suddenly, the couch and Netflix beat out your carefully planned evening routine.

Research backs all this up. Wendy Wood, who studies habit formation, found that relapse rates spike during transitions or stressful times when the environment changes or demands pile up (Wood et al., 2015). James Clear points out that even the most motivated people will revert to automatic behaviors if those behaviors are deeply wired and triggered by emotion or circumstance (Clear, n.d.). In fact, studies show that nearly 80% of people trying to break old patterns experience at least one significant relapse. You're not a statistic—you're human.

Here's what these triggers look like in real life. When deadlines pile up at work, you might promise yourself you'll just check Instagram for five minutes to "take the edge off." Those five minutes turn into an hour, and now guilt is tagging along for the ride. Or maybe you're dealing with a family emergency—your mind is scattered, so you put off even simple tasks, telling yourself you'll regroup tomorrow. Burnout after a stretch of high performance can be especially tricky— after weeks of being "on," your brain rebels, craving rest or distraction, and suddenly even easy habits feel impossible.

Relapse doesn't strike out of nowhere—it follows a cycle with clear stages. First comes the trigger: stress, exhaustion, or an unexpected disruption. Then the slip happens: a missed task here, an ignored calendar block there. Next comes the emotional response: frustration, guilt, shame. This is where things can get dangerous. If you start beating yourself up or catastrophizing ("I always do this," "I'll never change"), you risk escalation—slipping further into avoidance or even giving up completely.

Reflection Exercise: Map Your Own Relapse Cycle

Take a moment and think back to the last time you fell off track with a habit or routine that mattered to you. Close your eyes if it helps. What set it off? Was it stress from work, something happening at home, or just plain fatigue? What did you do differently: skip a workout, ignore your planner, binge on distractions? How did it feel emotionally? Were you frustrated, embarrassed, or annoyed with yourself? Finally, what happened next? Did you spiral further or eventually course-correct? Jot down each step as honestly as possible in a journal or notes app.

Here's how it might look:

- **Trigger:** Boss emails late at night with urgent requests.
- **Slip:** Skip planning my morning; hit snooze three times.
- **Emotional Response:** Feel guilty and overwhelmed.
- **Escalation:** Avoid my inbox all day, feel worse by evening.

By mapping your own cycle, you shine a light on the patterns that trip you up most often. This awareness doesn't fix everything overnight, but it's powerful—it gives you the clarity to spot relapse earlier next time and respond with kindness instead of criticism. If nothing else lands from this chapter, let it be this: relapse isn't the end—it's just part of building lasting change.

THE "FAST RESET" ROUTINE: WHAT TO DO WHEN YOU SLIP

When you realize you're off track—maybe you've missed calendar blocks or spent an hour cycling through tabs—it's easy to feel things are spiraling. That feeling can sneak up whether you're managing a budget, juggling family schedules, or just trying to survive a busy week. The urge to ignore the slip or punish yourself only keeps you stuck. What really helps is a simple, immediate reset—a small action, not a grand or overwhelming fix. I call this the "Fast Reset" routine. It's saved my productivity countless times.

The Fast Reset includes just three steps: **pause, acknowledge, act**. You don't need fancy tools or lots of time—just about sixty seconds and the willingness to stop the spiral. Start with **pause**. This isn't a fake pause —like scrolling your phone or wandering around—it's a true stop. Plant your feet, close your laptop if needed, and take three long, deep breaths. Say aloud or internally, "Okay—I'm noticing I just slipped." This snaps you out of autopilot, resets your nervous system, and lets you catch your breath. It's not about self-criticism—it's simply creating some space between the slip and your next move. Even in a busy environment, those three breaths can help ground you.

Then, **acknowledge**. Remind yourself that relapses are normal. They're not evidence of laziness or failure, just signs you're human and that habit-building is tough. Tell yourself, "This happens to everyone," or "Missing a block doesn't erase all my progress." If self-talk feels awkward, imagine what you'd say to a friend—it's likely more encouraging than what your inner critic offers. Even a sticky note that says, "It's normal to slip," can gently shift your mindset. Allow yourself to feel disappointment, but don't turn it into self-criticism. Focus on progress over perfection.

Finally, **act**: the most critical step. Do one tiny thing to regain momentum. Make it so small it's hard *not* to do. Maybe it's replying to one overdue email or moving a single task forward. If you missed a week of time-blocking, set a five-minute timer and just outline the next hour —not the whole day. For parents whose routines fell apart over a hectic weekend, return to your starting ritual—put on headphones and open your laptop, even if the kids are watching cartoons. If you're stuck, use the 2-Minute Rule from Chapter 3: pick the smallest task and finish it. What matters is taking any action, no matter the amount.

For visual thinkers or list lovers, make the process visible. Write these steps on a sticky note and keep them near your workstation:

1. **Pause:** Three deep breaths. Name what happened.
2. **Acknowledge:** Remind yourself that this is normal.
3. **Act:** Do one small thing now.

This note acts as both a permission slip and a gentle prompt—no drama required.

Here's how it looks in real life: Kristin, a project manager, built strong time-blocking habits, but a chaotic week of client meetings threw her off. By Friday, her plans were derailed, and she was tempted to abandon her system. Instead of rewriting her whole plan, she paused, took deep breaths, and quietly told herself, "This week was nuts. It's okay." She opened her calendar and blocked just one hour for focused work on Monday morning—a simple act, but enough to regain control.

Or Dave, a parent who kept up his morning routine until a busy weekend knocked him off course. Monday dawned, and he felt scattered. Rather than waiting for the "perfect" reset, he took his coffee to the home office, put on his favorite playlist, and spent three minutes reviewing priorities for the day. That small step didn't fix everything, but it gave him momentum to tackle one important task before noon.

Slips will happen. What matters is how quickly and kindly you step out of them. Instead of powering through or trying to erase mistakes, the Fast Reset gives you a way to recognize you're off track and gently steer yourself back with a doable action. Keep the checklist close and make it part of your workspace. With practice, these resets become second nature—a subtle superpower for anyone aiming to create meaningful change amid the messiness of real life.

PRACTICING SELF-COMPASSION AND BOUNCING BACK

After a setback, your mind often reaches for criticism instead of understanding. The inner critic rushes in, cataloging past failures and shaming you for slipping up. This response is typical for most people, but it doesn't help recovery. Dr. Kristin Neff's research on self-compassion shows that your self-talk after a mistake affects how fast you bounce back. Self-compassion isn't about excusing every mistake—it's about giving yourself the same kindness and patience you'd offer a struggling friend. Care, rather than criticism, helps you recover instead of staying stuck.

Begin by noticing your self-talk when you mess up. Is your first reaction harsh or shaming? If so, pause and ask, "Would I say this to a friend?" Likely not. Dr. Neff suggests replacing self-judgment with self-kindness. If you're beating yourself up over procrastination or missing a commitment, try placing your hand over your heart and telling yourself, "This is hard, but I'm learning. I can start again." This small act interrupts the "shame spiral," relaxes your body, and, according to research, calms your nervous system and renews your motivation.

Writing can also be a powerful tool. After a relapse or tough day, write yourself a self-compassion letter. Describe what happened plainly, acknowledge your real emotions—like disappointment or frustration—and then offer supportive words you'd say to someone else: "You wanted to stick to your routine, but it was a rough week. You're allowed to feel tired. You can try again." Even if it feels awkward, reading your words aloud can reduce shame and help normalize setbacks as a universal part of life.

Another helpful practice is a daily or weekly check-in, especially after things go wrong. Take two minutes before bed or while brushing your teeth to ask, "What did I handle well today, even if it wasn't perfect?" Perhaps you've sent one important email or attended a meeting when you'd rather not. Record what you did well, then reflect on one lesson you may have learned from a stumble: "I see that I avoid big projects when overwhelmed; maybe breaking them down will help." You're not making excuses—you're learning how to course correct without punishing yourself.

Small self-compassion rituals can make a difference. Choose one evening a week to forgive yourself for missed goals. Write a simple note: "I forgive myself for missing my deadline; I can start again tomorrow." Or record a gentle voice memo for yourself. Some people use sticky notes on their monitor—"Progress, not perfection"—as daily reminders and encouragement.

This approach works in real life. For instance, a freelancer I coached once missed a major deadline. Panic and shame hit her first, and she felt like quitting, but she tried something new—she wrote a forgiveness letter to herself about the missed deadline and how she felt, reminded herself that one slip didn't undo her years of good work, and reached out to her client honestly. By responding with responsibility but not self-blame, she repaired the relationship and got back on track faster than if she'd stayed stuck in shame.

The key takeaway: self-compassion is practical resilience, not indulgence. It helps you see mistakes as information, not evidence of your flaws. Each time you show yourself kindness over criticism, you strengthen your ability to recover. With practice, responding with care starts to feel more natural and less forced (Neff, n.d.).

Try this now:

1. Write down something that didn't go well.
2. Name how it made you feel—honestly.
3. Imagine what you'd say to a friend in the same situation.
4. Write those words and read them aloud.

Being kind to yourself may feel strange at first; many of us learned to be hardest on ourselves. But with time, kind words become genuine, and that shift is key to getting up after setbacks—again and again—without shame holding you back.

You'll still hear that old inner critic sometimes, but each self-compassionate response loosens its hold. That's real resilience—measured by how you treat yourself when no one is watching.

SPOTTING EARLY WARNING SIGNS AND SETTING UP "TRIPWIRES"

You've probably noticed that relapses don't just happen out of nowhere. There are always little hints, subtle signals that your momentum is slipping. The trick is learning to spot these early warning signs, those tiny clues that you're about to fall back into old patterns. For many people, it starts with a change in energy or mood. You wake up already tired or find yourself feeling snappy at every tiny inconvenience. Suddenly, you're finding excuses to do anything except the task you meant to tackle. Maybe you start cleaning your kitchen instead of prepping for a big meeting, or you catch yourself scrolling mindlessly through social media when you promised yourself you'd start that report. These aren't random behaviors. They're signals—a little nudge from your mind that something's off and you're drifting toward avoidance.

These signals aren't always dramatic. Sometimes they're as simple as feeling unusually restless at your desk or spacing out during meetings. Maybe you keep putting off small decisions, telling yourself you'll "get to it later." Or perhaps your group chat notifications become impossible to resist just as you sit down to focus. It's easy to brush off these patterns as quirks, but they're your brain's way of waving a yellow flag. If you're honest with yourself, you can likely recall your own go-to avoidance moves—the little things you do when stress or fatigue starts to creep in. For some, it's organizing files that don't need organizing; for others, it's binge-watching videos, snacking, or even picking fights at home over nothing.

The challenge is catching these patterns before they spiral. That's where tripwires come in—this is a concept borrowed from business and decision-making circles but perfect for personal productivity. A tripwire is just a pre-set cue that prompts action the moment you notice an early warning sign. Think of it as an alert system, not a punishment. The minute you recognize an old avoidance behavior or emotional shift, your tripwire kicks in. It reminds you to do something different, even if it's small.

For example, if you know your first sign of relapse is endlessly refreshing your inbox without actually answering emails, set a digital tripwire: create a calendar event at 11 a.m. labeled "Inbox Reset." When the alert pops up, use it as your cue to pause and decide what truly needs your attention right now. Or maybe you tend to get irritable and tired just before slipping into procrastination—stick a neon note on your bathroom mirror: "Feeling off? Take five and check in." The goal is to catch yourself before things snowball—not to pile on guilt.

Many professionals rely on these kinds of reminders to keep themselves honest. One remote worker I know sets a pop-up notification for noon every single day: if she hasn't finished at least one priority task by then, the pop-up tells her to step away from her screen, stretch, and review her focus list before lunch. She swears it stops her from drifting into unproductive afternoons. Another friend who juggles work and parenting uses a daily alarm on her phone labeled "Check-In." When it goes off (usually right before school pickup), she takes two minutes to ask herself, "Have I made progress on my main goal today?" If not, she adjusts her plans for the evening: sometimes moving tasks, sometimes recruiting help, and sometimes just permitting herself to let go for the day.

Setting up tripwires doesn't have to be complicated or high-tech. Sticky notes on your monitor can serve as visual nudges: "Are you working or just looking busy?" If you tend to avoid big projects by getting lost in admin work, schedule a recurring 2 p.m. calendar reminder called "Big Task Check." It's a small interruption meant to jolt you out of autopilot. For those who thrive on accountability, recruit a friend or colleague and agree to text each other every Thursday morning: "What's your frog today?" This ritual forces both of you to name your biggest avoidance target and commit to tackling it (Ang, 2022).

Here's an exercise to make this practical for your own life:

Warning Signs & Tripwires Mapping Worksheet

1. **List Your Warning Signs:** Write down the specific behaviors, thoughts, or feelings that usually show up right before you relapse into procrastination or avoidance. Get specific: think "refreshing inbox every five minutes," "arguing with my partner over chores," "rearranging my bookshelf," or "feeling tired for no clear reason."
2. **Choose Your Tripwires:** For each warning sign, brainstorm one simple tripwire—a cue, reminder, or nudge—to intercept the behavior. Examples: calendar pop-ups ("Focus reset"), sticky notes ("Pause and check priorities"), alarms ("Two-minute movement break"), or buddy check-ins.
3. **Place Your Tripwires:** Set them up where you'll see them at the right time—on your phone, laptop, bathroom mirror, fridge door, or even in your car.

4. **Review Weekly:** End each week by checking which tripwires
   worked and which didn't fire when needed. Adjust as your
   patterns shift.

You're not looking for perfection; just enough awareness so that when
those old behaviors sneak in, you can meet them with action instead of
regret. You're simply giving your future self a fighting chance on even
the most hectic days.

TURNING SETBACKS INTO INSIGHT—REAL-WORLD CASE STUDIES

Not every stumble is a disaster. Sometimes, it's the crack in your
perfect plan that allows you to truly learn something. I've seen this
play out again and again, both in my own life and in the lives of
people I've worked with. Take Anna, a marketing lead in a fast-
growing startup. She'd been riding the high of several strong
campaigns, feeling like she'd finally cracked her procrastination habits.
Then came a launch that tanked—deadlines were missed, small details
slipped through the cracks, and the whole team ended up scrambling
at the last minute. Anna could have let this confirm her old story—that
she'd always fall back into old patterns under pressure. Instead, she
pressed pause and got curious. She reviewed her project notes, flagged
every missed step, and realized she'd been relying too much on
memory and last-minute energy. The turning point was humility—she
admitted to herself that her usual approach wasn't working with
bigger, more complex projects.

From this low point, Anna started experimenting with project planning
tools. She tried a weekly review, breaking down each launch into
smaller milestones with clear deadlines, and she set up regular check-
in meetings with her team. The next campaign didn't just go smoother
—it felt less stressful from start to finish. Anna told me later, "I never
thought failure would be what finally made me change how I plan
projects. Now, every time something goes sideways, I ask myself what
I can build or tweak so it doesn't happen twice." The insight here is
simple but powerful: notice your relapse pattern in detail, and use it as
feedback, not a final verdict.

Now consider Marcus, an attorney who always prided himself on his organization until one day he missed a filing deadline, a mistake that couldn't be fixed with a late-night email. Instead of spiraling into self-criticism, Marcus decided to map out exactly where things broke down. He saw that his old system—a long to-do list—wasn't cutting it as his client load grew. Rather than sticking with what was comfortable, he decided to overhaul his workflow. He spent a weekend learning about Kanban boards, the kind that let him move tasks from "To Do" to "In Progress" to "Done." At first, it felt awkward and clunky. However, after a few weeks, he noticed he was seeing his bottlenecks in real time and prioritizing better. The big win? He not only prevented missed deadlines but also started finishing work ahead of schedule for the first time in years.

Both Anna and Marcus faced the kind of setbacks that make you want to crawl under your desk and hide. What changed everything for them wasn't superhuman willpower—it was their willingness to treat failure as information. Each one paused after their relapse, got honest about what went wrong (without sugarcoating or shaming), and then took action to build a better system for next time. They made their reset routines non-negotiable and used tools that matched their real needs instead of sticking with what felt safe.

If you're reading this after a setback—maybe you missed a goal at work or let your personal habits slide—consider taking a page from these stories. Instead of beating yourself up or pretending nothing happened, try treating your stumble as raw data. Ask yourself: What did this reveal about my triggers? Was it a lack of planning, too much on my plate, or something else? What small experiment could you run next time to make relapse less likely or easier to spot early? Maybe it's trying a new app for tracking progress, scheduling regular check-ins with a coworker, or simply writing down your biggest tasks every morning before email takes over.

Here's a prompt you can use after your next setback: "What did this setback reveal about my triggers? What will I try next time?" Grab your notebook or open your favorite notes app and free-write for five minutes. Don't edit yourself or sugarcoat; just be honest.

Setbacks don't have to be clean rebounds every time; they can be ways to collect lessons as you move forward, so each relapse nudges you toward better systems and more self-awareness. Anna's failed launch became the seed for better planning; Marcus's missed deadline forced him to adopt a tool that now saves him hours each week. Your own story can shift, too—if you let setbacks be teachers instead of judges.

As you reach the end of this chapter, remember: relapse isn't a dead end but an invitation to adjust and grow. The next chapter will show how to personalize these strategies so your productivity systems fit your real life—even when things get messy again.

CHAPTER 9
CUSTOMIZING YOUR PROCRASTINATION SOLUTION FOR REAL LIFE

SOLUTIONS FOR REMOTE WORKERS AND HOME OFFICE DISTRACTIONS

Working from home might sound freeing, but distractions lurk everywhere. Your workspace could be a kitchen table stacked with chores within sight, or a couch where the urge to start dinner hits hours early. No commute means no natural start or stop to your day, so it's easy to blur the lines between work and leisure. You might find yourself checking Slack while folding towels or letting your work hours stretch late because you lack a clear endpoint. Isolation can also sap motivation, making it challenging to stay on track, especially without colleagues to remind you of goals or break the monotony. With household chores competing for attention, and the kitchen always in reach, it's easy to end up snacking, meal prepping, or cleaning instead of finishing your project.

This isn't just about willpower—your environment shapes habits. Without physical boundaries or the commute to an office, you'll need to create your own structure. Even without a separate office, designate a focused work area. A portable work caddy can turn any corner into a temporary office. Fill it with your essentials: a laptop, charger, pens, sticky notes, maybe a small lamp. Set up your caddy in a chosen spot—a specific chair, a part of the table, or windowsill—to create a sense of transition from "home" to "work." Visible cues help others respect your work time—like a "work in session" sign or a simple color code system (green for interruptible, red for not, for example) if you share your space. Over time, these signals become routine and help reduce interruptions.

Your remote workday needs structure beyond simply being busy. Block time specifically for uninterrupted focus—your personal "door closed" hours—even if there's no actual door. Establish clear start and end times. Begin with a ritual to signal that work has started, like making a certain tea or putting on headphones. Mimic office routines by building in breaks; walk around the block, stretch, or just leave the room for a minute. These transitions act as mental resets, helping you mark progress and avoid burnout.

Setting and communicating boundaries is essential when your home is your office. Use simple scripts to clarify availability without guilt. For family: "I'll be working until noon—let's talk after?" For your team, update your status (like "Heads down—deep work until 11 a.m.") so colleagues know not to expect immediate replies. If you're concerned about missing something urgent, let others know when you'll check in next: "I'll respond after lunch." For clients, set up an out-of-office message when you need uninterrupted focus: "I'm currently working offline and will reply after 2 p.m." Small steps like these reduce miscommunication and help protect your focus (Spill Chat, n.d.).

Interactive Element: Remote Work Distraction Audit

Try this quick exercise: Draw two columns on paper or in a note. On the left, list all distractions from your last remote workday—be specific (such as "checked phone," "chatted with roommate," "folded laundry," "got coffee three times"). On the right, write one change you could make for each: put your phone across the room, schedule conversations, prep snacks ahead of time. Pick two to test tomorrow. Notice what changes; a simple tweak can create surprising relief.

Ultimately, remote work isn't about perfect focus every day. Aim to set signals that fit your needs and communicate clearly with those around you. Focus on building just enough structure and clarity to consistently get work done, without letting home distractions steal your day. Progress, not perfection, is the goal.

ADAPTING TOOLS FOR PARENTS, CAREGIVERS, AND COMPLEX LIVES

Life as a parent or caregiver rarely fits the neat mold shown in productivity articles with flawless planners and color-coded journals. Your reality is an unpredictable jumble of work deadlines, school emails, unexpected needs, and grocery lists you'll forget unless you jot them down immediately. You might squeeze in work during nap times or after school drop-off, only to have plans derailed by a fever or a last-minute call from the nurse. Your time is hardly your own—it's borrowed, bartered, and constantly interrupted. Often, it feels like all you can do is hold things together.

Rigid routines or long, peaceful blocks of time are out of reach—flexibility is essential. Color-coding tasks by urgency and flexibility helps clarify what needs immediate attention and what can wait. For instance, assign red to "must-do today," yellow to "do soon if possible," and blue to "nice to do when there's time." Keep this color system on your phone, fridge, or planner where you'll regularly see it. When chaos strikes, focus on the red tasks—no wasted energy deciding what's most important. Think of your morning is a menu of options. If the kids get up early, maybe you just grab coffee and check a few emails. If you get an unexpected half hour, use it for something more involved. Each part of your routine can stand alone, ready to be paused or replaced as needed.

Fragmented time—snippets of five minutes here, seven minutes there—is the norm. Don't wait for a solid hour of focus; instead, keep a "just start" list of micro-tasks handy. These small actions, like replying to a message, scanning a receipt, jotting down a single idea, or scheduling an appointment online, might not seem like much, but they add up. Keep this list easily accessible, like on your phone or a sticky note, and you'll be surprised how much progress you make over a week by jumping on these gaps.

Many parents and caregivers get creative with their tools. For example, a single dad records voice memos in the carpool line, outlining work ideas while he waits, then transcribes them at home. Another caregiver uses waiting rooms during medical appointments to batch emails or catch up on digital chores. These methods aren't glamorous, but they turn otherwise wasted minutes into small, low-stress wins.

It's common to feel guilty for "not doing more" or to compare yourself to colleagues with fewer demands at home. Let go of these comparisons—your circumstances are different, and so are your victories. Even brief moments of progress, like sending a crucial email during a nap or prepping a report between loads of laundry, build momentum. When plans get derailed, simply check your color-coded list and tackle the most urgent task—no need to dwell on what didn't get done.

Journaling can help, not as a burden, but as a tool to spot patterns and celebrate what actually worked. Once a week, jot down when you found surprise pockets of time and what tasks fit best into those blocks. With time, you'll see which strategies help you chip away at bigger projects or navigate daily demands.

If you're balancing caring for others—children, elderly parents, or anyone who depends on you— alongside work, give yourself permission to adapt any tool until it fits your messy, unpredictable life. No system is too simple if it helps you handle another day with less stress and more self-kindness (Thompson, 2025).

MANAGING PROCRASTINATION WITH ANXIETY, ADHD, OR NEURODIVERSITY

Living with anxiety, ADHD, or any other type of neurodivergent mind changes how procrastination shows up for you. It's not a matter of laziness or weak willpower; your brain plays by different rules. You might get lost in thought, struggle to start even the smallest task, or feel overwhelmed by the sheer act of planning. Executive function, which is the brain's ability to manage initiation, organize steps, and keep attention on track, can feel like it's working against you. This isn't a character flaw. It's a neurological reality, and you're not alone.

If you live with ADHD or are neurodivergent in any way, time can become slippery. Hours disappear without warning. You might plan to start a report after lunch, only to look up and see the sun setting. This "time blindness" is a classic sign—your mind isn't tracking the clock the way others do. Visual timers can be a lifesaver. Instead of relying on your phone's numbers, try a timer with a colored dial or digital countdown that shows time shrinking. Place it where you work. The changing visuals keep you anchored in the present moment and help break work into manageable chunks. Set it for 15 or 25 minutes, then take a break. Reset as needed—don't worry about sticking to some perfect schedule.

For those who crave stimulation, working in silence might feel like pure torture. If your mind starts to wander or anxiety creeps in, experiment with environmental anchors. Fidget tools—like stress balls, smooth stones, or even a textured pen—offer sensory input to occupy restless hands without pulling focus from your work. Background music or ambient noise (think lo-fi beats or rain sounds) can block distractions and create a rhythm for your brain to follow. Some people even find comfort in weighted blankets or a favorite hoodie; these tactile cues calm the nervous system and make it easier to settle in.

Body doubling is another powerful tool for neurodivergent brains. You don't need a coworker physically present; even working on video with a friend or joining a virtual coworking session can make tasks feel less overwhelming. Sometimes another person's silent presence is enough to spark focus—no conversation necessary. This method works because of accountability and shared energy—not because you're socializing.

Energy and attention fluctuate wildly for many neurodivergent folks. For some, late-night hours bring clarity while the world sleeps. If that's true for you, don't fight it. Lean into those quiet sprints when your mind feels sharpest, even if it means working unconventional hours (within reason). Others might need frequent movement breaks, not just as a luxury but as a necessity to reset brain chemistry and shake off restlessness. Give yourself permission to move—stand up, pace, do ten jumping jacks—without apology. These breaks aren't distractions; they're part of your productivity toolkit.

Communicating your needs can feel intimidating, especially if you worry about judgment or misunderstanding from colleagues or supervisors. Scripts make these conversations less awkward. Suppose you need deadline flexibility due to ADHD. In that case, an email can be as simple as: "I do my best work with clear structure and sometimes need extra time for complex projects due to how my brain processes tasks—can we discuss some flexibility around this deadline?" When talking with partners or accountability buddies, try: "I focus better with check-ins or reminders—would you be willing to help by sending a quick text when you're starting your work?" For coworkers: "Here's what helps me stay on track: regular updates, clear next steps, and written reminders instead of verbal ones."

Some days will be messy, and progress will be uneven. On those days, self-compassion matters more than ever. Recognize that neurodiverse brains work in cycles—sometimes hyper-focused and wildly productive, other times scattered and slow-moving. Instead of aiming for consistency that looks like everyone else's, track your own patterns and lean into what works for you. Keep tools visible and routines flexible. Celebrate every small victory: a finished email, a completed slide, even just opening the file that scares you most. Over time, these strategies stack up into progress that fits your real life and works with your brain (Mental Health America, 2024).

WHAT TO DO WHEN MOTIVATION AND ENERGY CRASH

Motivation doesn't just dip; it sometimes vanishes without warning, leaving you staring at your screen, mind blank, hands heavy. If you've ever sat wondering why you can't get moving even on things you care about, you're not alone. These slumps hit harder than small afternoon lulls. You might notice your body feels leaden, or that even the idea of responding to a simple email feels enormous. Sometimes you start skipping meals or sleep, feeling detached or short-tempered. You may find yourself zoning out more often or dreading tasks that were once routine. When energy and drive tank this way, it's usually more than laziness—it's your body and mind sending up a flare. Burnout, physical exhaustion, or decision overload can flatten even the most driven person. The warning signs are subtle at first: a headache that lingers, a tightness in your chest as you open your calendar, or a creeping sense that everything is "just too much." Ignore those signs for long enough, and they build into a full-blown shutdown.

When you reach this point, shift into what I call "triage mode." Stop expecting yourself to run at full speed. Instead, zero in on survival: what are the top one or two things that absolutely must get done today? Make a tiny checklist—literally two boxes max. Give yourself permission to drop, delay, or reschedule everything else. This isn't failure—it's smart resource management. If you're swamped at work and home, or your brain refuses to cooperate, focus only on the basics: maybe it's answering that urgent client message or prepping food for your family. That's it. Lower the bar until success feels possible, even when motivation is gone.

Gentle re-engagement matters more than brute force. Sometimes the best way to restart isn't by leaping in but by moving your body for five minutes—what I call movement snacks. Stretch your arms over your head, walk from one end of your place to the other, or just step outside for air. This isn't exercise—it's a physical reset. If your head feels foggy, try a mini digital detox: close your laptop, silence notifications, and step away from screens for ten or fifteen minutes. These pauses aren't wasted time—they're ways to reset cognitive fatigue and allow your system to breathe. Often, after just a small break, tasks shrink back to size and the urge to procrastinate lessens.

Self-forgiveness is crucial during these crashes. It's easy to spiral into guilt—telling yourself you're lazy or unreliable—but that narrative only deepens the rut. Talk to yourself as you would a friend: "Hey, it's okay that I feel off right now. I'll do what I can and try again tomorrow." (See Chapter 8 for more insights on "self-compassion") Sometimes self-talk isn't enough. If you notice that these slumps last for weeks instead of days, or if you feel hopeless, disconnected from things you usually love, or can't seem to rest no matter how much you try, it might be time to reach out for help.

There's no shame in asking for support—sometimes energy crashes signal something deeper. If your body aches constantly, sleep never seems refreshing, or anxiety and sadness are sticking around, think about making an appointment with a doctor or therapist. It's okay to say to a friend, "I'm struggling with motivation lately and don't know why—can we talk?" Or send a message like, "Things have felt off for a while, and I need someone to listen." Most people want to help but don't know you need it unless you tell them.

Energy and motivation are not endless resources—they ebb and flow, influenced by stress, life changes, health issues, and emotional weight. The key is learning to work with these natural rhythms instead of fighting them. This means spotting the difference between a normal lull and a real crash, then responding appropriately. When things get rough, scale back your expectations, do the bare minimum without guilt, take care of your body first, and ask for backup when you need it. These choices aren't admissions of defeat—they're signs of wisdom and self-respect in action (Harvard Health Publishing, 2023).

CREATING YOUR ONGOING PROGRESS PLAYBOOK

Building a playbook for your ongoing progress is like making a personal cheat sheet for real life. It's a place where you gather the tactics, reminders, and tools that work for you, not just what sounds good in theory. You've tried dozens of strategies by now. Some fell flat, but a few stuck. It's time to keep those wins in one spot. Whether you grab a blank notebook or set up a digital document, start by listing your top five personal go-to moves—these might be "write a two-minute email to break inertia," "use my playlist for focus," or "do a brain dump when I freeze." The goal isn't to build a masterpiece—it's to create something you'll use. Print your playbook and stick it where you'll see it: above your desk, on the fridge, or on your phone's home screen. If you prefer more digital tools, set calendar reminders with links to your playbook, or create a widget for quick access.

A playbook needs to stay alive. Life doesn't sit still—your obstacles and routines won't either. Make it a habit to check in with yourself once a month. Set a reminder on your calendar: "Playbook check." Ask yourself what's working right now. What feels stale? Maybe you notice that your "reward stack" isn't motivating anymore, or your quick-win list needs a refresh. If you've had a stretch of good days, jot down what helped and add it to your playbook before it slips away. On rough weeks, write down what tripped you up, then brainstorm tweaks or new tactics to try. Your playbook is a living document, not a rulebook set in stone.

Keeping your playbook visible and accessible is key. Place a printed version on your desk or tape it inside your planner. If you live in Google Calendar, create a recurring event called "Check Playbook" and paste the latest version into the notes field. For those using habit tracker apps, add "review my playbook" as a weekly habit. The more often you see your strategies, the more likely you are to use them, especially when stress hits and old habits try to take over.

Different roles and different brains call for different playbooks. For a remote worker, the list might include: "my reset routine: three deep breaths and one stretch break every hour," "reward stack: treat myself to five minutes of music after finishing hard tasks," and "quick-win micro-tasks: reply to urgent emails before lunch." A parent's playbook may be more fluid: "reset routine: move laundry while thinking through work priorities," "reward stack: coffee after school drop-off if I finish a key call," and "quick-win list: schedule doctor appointments during cartoons." For a neurodivergent adult, their playbook could feature: "reset routine: change rooms when stuck," "reward stack: sticker chart for small wins," and "micro-tasks: set visual timer for 10-minute sprints."

Playbook Integration Checklist

- Print or save your playbook in an easy-to-find spot.
- Schedule a monthly review and set up an alert.
- Add your playbook link or excerpt to your calendar or notes app.
- Update after every big win or tough week.
- Keep it simple and swap out strategies as life changes.

During your monthly check-in, you can also use journaling prompts, like "Which tactic helped me bounce back this month?" or "What habit did I stop using—and why?" This process only takes five minutes, but it can save you hours of frustration and second-guessing later. Building this habit means you're always prepared with strategies that fit your current reality, not some idealized version of yourself.

A progress playbook is not about perfection; it's about staying flexible, self-aware, and equipped for whatever life throws at you next.

As you wrap up this chapter and look ahead, remember: procrastination looks different for everyone, and your solution must fit your real life. Setbacks aren't failures—they're data. Treat yourself with the same compassion you'd offer a friend, keep experimenting with what works, and trust that progress, not perfection, is the goal.

KEEPING THE MOMENTUM ALIVE

You've done something remarkable. You've learned to spot your triggers, built your toolkit, and discovered that procrastination isn't a character flaw —it's just a pattern that can be changed. You know what it feels like to finally take action instead of putting things off until tomorrow.

Now you have everything you need to break free from procrastination and build unstoppable productivity. But here's the thing: **someone else is still stuck in that same frustrating loop you just escaped.**

Right now, someone is staring at their screen, feeling overwhelmed, wondering if they'll ever get their act together. They're beating themselves up for missing another deadline or putting off another important task. **They're where you were before you picked up this book.**

Your review could be the nudge that changes everything for them.

Why Your Review Matters

- Real people need real solutions – your experience shows others what's possible
- Busy professionals are searching for strategies that actually work in messy, real life
- Your story could be the encouragement someone needs to finally take action

Simply by leaving your honest opinion, you'll **show other busy professionals, overwhelmed parents, and anyone tired of feeling tired of falling behind where they can find the help they're looking for.** You'll help them discover that productivity doesn't have to be punishment—it can actually feel good.

Maybe you only used one or two strategies from this book. Maybe you're still working on building your habits. That's perfectly fine. **Share what worked for you, even if it was just one small win. Your real experience matters more than perfection.**

What You May Want to Include in Your Review

- Which specific strategy made the biggest difference for you
- How your daily productivity has changed

- What you wish you'd known about procrastination before reading this book
- Who would benefit most from these tools

Scan the QR code to leave your review and help someone else get unstuck.

Already left a review? Consider sharing the book with a colleague, friend, or family member who's struggling with procrastination. Sometimes the best gift is helping someone else discover they're not alone—and that change is absolutely possible.

Thank you for reading, for taking action, and for helping others discover they're not broken, just human. The fight against procrastination stays alive when we pass on our knowledge—and you're proving that procrastination doesn't have to win.

Bobby L. Butler

"Progress, not perfection. Action, not excuses. You've got this."

CONCLUSION

Let's be honest: finishing a book on procrastination is a win in itself. You could have put this down at any point, but you didn't. That says a lot about you. It means you're not just someone who dreams about change—you're someone who takes real steps, even when they're messy or imperfect. That's what this whole journey is about.

I want you to hear this, loud and clear: overcoming procrastination and building unstoppable productivity is 100% possible for you. Not because you suddenly wake up a different person, but because you now have a toolbox packed with daily, practical strategies that actually work in real life. You've learned that real productivity comes from understanding your brain, giving yourself what you really need, and moving forward one small, doable step at a time—not from grinding harder or shaming yourself into action.

Let's look back at where you started and how far you've come, even if it doesn't always feel like a leap. We began by stripping away the old, heavy myth that procrastination is laziness. We saw it for what it is—a habit loop, rooted in our psychology and biology, not a personal failure. You discovered your unique procrastination archetype through the diagnostic quiz, learning whether you're a Perfectionist who gets stuck in endless editing, an Overwhelmed Avoider who freezes when projects feel too big, a Thrill-Seeker who needs deadline pressure to focus, or a Decision Paralysis type who gets lost in too many options. You learned to replace vague guilt with specific self-awareness.

From there, you learned to spot your real obstacles—the specific triggers, distractions, and emotional patterns that activate your procrastination archetype. You mapped out what overwhelms you, whether it's perfectionism paralysis when "good enough" feels impossible, decision fatigue from too many choices, digital distractions that fragment your attention, or the guilt and shame spirals that keep you stuck. You took your personal distraction audit and learned to identify the difference between urgent interruptions and important focus work. Most importantly, you discovered that fear of feedback often keeps you frozen, and that awareness of that alone began to loosen its grip.

Then you built momentum with quick-win tactics. You practiced the 2-minute rule, knocking out easy tasks to get the ball rolling. You discovered the power of micro-tasks—breaking big, scary projects into tiny, specific steps. You tried brain dumps to clear the mental clutter and make action possible. You learned to "eat the frog" and tackle the hardest thing first, even when it felt uncomfortable.

Next, you built your own anti-procrastination toolkit. You set up Kanban boards and visual trackers to see your progress, because our brains love visible wins. You gave time-blocking a real shot—on your own terms. You batched similar tasks to protect your energy, and you experimented with Pomodoro sprints to transform focus into a game of short, achievable bursts. You even wrestled your inbox into submission, proving that chaos can be tamed.

Motivation became something you could engineer, not just hope for. You stacked rewards, celebrated tiny victories, and used implementation intentions to turn good intentions into action. You made boring tasks more satisfying through gamification and habit hacks. Most important, you connected your daily actions to your deeper values— the "why" that makes even routine tasks meaningful.

You learned that routines don't have to be rigid or perfect to stick. You designed modular mornings, used reset blocks after bad days, and planned your weeks with action ladders and priority maps. You learned to build white space into your schedule and to reboot your routines after travel, sickness, or setbacks—no guilt required.

And you didn't do it alone. You saw the power of accountability—whether through a buddy, self-contracts, digital trackers, or honest community. You saw that willpower gets you started, but connection keeps you going.

We didn't shy away from the messy parts, either. We talked about relapse. We named it. We made fast resets and self-compassion part of your toolbox. You learned to spot your early warning signs and set up "tripwires" before things spiral. You saw that every setback is actually a chance to learn, tweak, and come back stronger.

The most powerful strategies from this book—micro-tasks, the 2-minute rule, brain dumps, Kanban boards, Pomodoro sprints, modular and flexible routines, reset blocks, accountability buddies, and digital trackers—are all here for you to use, adapt, and remix as your life changes. None of these tools are one-size-fits-all. Your system should look like your life, your brain, your schedule. The best productivity plan is the one you'll actually use and adjust as you go.

I hope, more than anything, you feel the freedom to be kind to yourself. Self-compassion is not a luxury here—it's the fuel. You don't have to earn the right to forgive yourself for a rough day, a missed deadline, or a week when nothing went as planned. Reflection and self-forgiveness will always carry you farther than shame. Progress beats perfection, every single time.

If you've made it this far, I hope you take a second to celebrate. You've done the hard part—you've shown up, you've been honest, and you've tried. Every exercise you finished, every trigger you named, every tiny win you celebrated—they all count. Momentum isn't made of grand gestures but from small, stubborn steps, repeated more days than not.

My encouragement is simple: keep experimenting. Treat your productivity as a series of mini science projects. Tweak your routines. Drop what doesn't work. Try new strategies as your life changes. And when you slip (because you will), don't give up. Reset, reflect, and take the next tiny step. If you need help, reach out—don't isolate.

Here's my final, heartfelt ask: pick one thing from this book—just one. It might be a start ritual, a brain dump, or a quick reset after a tough morning. Do it today. Mark it as done. Celebrate it, no matter how small. That's your first step toward building a life where procrastination doesn't call the shots.

Lasting change isn't about avoiding slips, doubts, or overwhelm. It's about getting up, again and again, and taking the next small action. You are not alone in this. Your story isn't finished. Every step you take is a new beginning.

Let's see what you can do. Your next action could change everything.

REFERENCES

- Abdaal, A. (2024, December 20). 5 Ways to gamify your tasks and get work done faster. *Ali Abdaal*. https://aliabdaal.com/productivity/5-ways-to-gamify-your-tasks-and-get-work-done-faster/
- Ang, N. (2022, February 21). Set tripwires for yourself to make better decisions. *Medium*. https://medium.com/re-engineering/set-tripwires-for-yourself-to-make-better-decisions-3b37a3aa3f70
- Boogaard, K. (2019, January 3). What's microproductivity? The small habit that will lead you to big wins. *Atlassian Blog*. https://www.atlassian.com/blog/productivity/microproductivity-break-tasks-into-smaller-steps
- Boogaard, K. (2023, December 8). Decision fatigue: What to do when endless choices are sapping your energy. *Atlassian Blog*. https://www.atlassian.com/blog/productivity/decision-fatigue
- Boyes, A. (2020, March 3). Don't let perfection be the enemy of productivity. *Harvard Business Review*. https://hbr.org/2020/03/dont-let-perfection-be-the-enemy-of-productivity
- Braithwaite, L. (n.d.). Why do we make worse decisions at the end of the day? Decision fatigue, explained. *The Decision Lab*. https://thedecisionlab.com/biases/decision-fatigue
- Chaudhuri, A. (2023, November 27). The buddy boost: How 'accountability partners' make you healthy, happy and more successful. *The Guardian*. https://www.theguardian.com/lifeandstyle/2023/nov/27/the-buddy-boost-how-accountability-partners-make-you-healthy-happy-and-more-successful
- Chen, V. (2024, May 2). The brain dump: Your guide to mental clarity. *Motion Blog*. https://www.usemotion.com/blog/brain-dump
- Clear, J. (n.d.). How to stop procrastinating by using the "2-minute rule." *James Clear*. https://jamesclear.com/how-to-stop-procrastinating
- Ferrari, J. R. (2020, October 16). The prevalence of procrastination. *Psychology Today*. https://www.psychologytoday.com/us/blog/still-procrastinating/202010/the-prevalence-procrastination
- Fogg, B. J. (2020, January 6). How you can use the power of celebration to make new habits stick. *TED Ideas*. https://ideas.ted.com/how-you-can-use-the-power-of-celebration-to-make-new-habits-stick/
- Gelwicks, A. (2024, February 15). Boost productivity with Kanban boards: The science-backed benefits. *Gelwick's Tech Articles*. https://www.gelwickstech.com/articles/2024/2/14/boost-productivity-with-kanban-boards-the-science-backed-benefits
- George, T. (2023, October 17). Eat the frog: Does it make you more productive? *MeisterTask Blog*. https://www.meistertask.com/blog/eat-the-frog
- Harvard Health Publishing. (2023, April 12). Boosting energy & managing

fatigue. *Harvard Health.* https://www.health.harvard.edu/topics/energy-and-fatigue

- Insights Psychology. (2024, November 29). Procrastination and the brain: A neuroscience guide. *Insights Psychology.* https://insightspsychology.org/the-neuroscience-of-procrastination/

- Kelley, S. (2018, June 6). It's about time: Immediate rewards boost motivation. *Cornell Chronicle.* https://news.cornell.edu/stories/2018/06/its-about-time-immediate-rewards-boost-motivation

- Laoyan, S. (2025, January 7). How task batching can increase your productivity at work. *Asana Resources.* https://asana.com/resources/task-batching

- Lemay, N. (n.d.). Rethinking productivity: Adapting the Pomodoro technique to your work style. *Life at Blog.* https://lifeat.io/blog/rethinking-productivity-adapting-the-pomodoro-technique-to-your-work-style

- Lieberman, C. (2019, March 25). Why you procrastinate (it has nothing to do with self-control). *The New York Times.* https://www.nytimes.com/2019/03/25/smarter-living/why-you-procrastinate-it-has-nothing-to-do-with-self-control.html

- Mental Health America. (2024, December 11). Working from home with ADHD. *MHA Learning Hub.* https://mhanational.org/learning-hub/working-from-home-with-adhd/

- Michal, K. (2020, October 15). The best morning habits for those who aren't morning people. *The Ladders.* https://www.theladders.com/career-advice/the-best-morning-habits-for-those-who-arent-morning-people

- Miss Unconventional. (n.d.). How to bounce back from a setback: Step 4 rest, reset, reload. *Miss Unconventional.* https://missunconventional.com/how-to-bounce-back-from-a-setback-step-4-rest-reset-reload/

- Neff, K. (n.d.). Self-compassion practices. *Self-Compassion.org.* https://self-compassion.org/self-compassion-practices/

- Rosen, L. & Samuel, A. (2015, June). Conquering digital distraction. *Harvard Business Review.* https://hbr.org/2015/06/conquering-digital-distraction

- Scroggs, L. (2024). Time blocking: And its task batching and day theming. Control your schedule so it doesn't control you. *Todoist.* https://www.todoist.com/productivity-methods/time-blocking

- Shatz, I. (n.d.). Why people procrastinate: The psychology and causes of procrastination. *Solving Procrastination Newsletter.* https://solvingprocrastination.com/why-people-procrastinate/

- Spill Chat. (n.d.). Focusing while working from home. *Spill Chat.* https://www.spill.chat/questions/struggling-to-focus

- Sumrell, M. (2024). 3 Planning systems to stop overwhelm in its tracks. *Work + Life Harmony Newsletter.* https://www.megansumrell.com/blog/3-planning-systems-to-stop-overwhelm-in-its-tracks

- Thompson, S. (2025, May 9). Overcoming procrastination during parental duties. *Ahead App Blog.* https://ahead-app.com/blog/procrastination/overcoming-procrastination-during-parental-duties-breaking-free-from-delay

- Wieber, F., Thurmer, J. L., & Gollwitzer, P. M. (2015, July 14). Promoting the translation of intentions into action by implementation intentions. *PMC*. https://pmc.ncbi.nlm.nih.gov/articles/PMC4500900/

- Wilde, K. (2023, February 16). Running an online community: 7 key pillars to success. *Teach:able Blog*. https://teachable.com/blog/how-to-run-online-community
- Wood, W., Labrecque, J. S., Lin, P., & Runger, D. (2023). Habits in dual process models. *USC Dornsife - Wendy Wood*. https://dornsife.usc.edu/wendy-wood/wp-content/uploads/sites/183/2023/10/Habits_in_Dual_Process_Models.pdf
- Wood, W. & Runger, D. (2015, September 10). Psychology of habit. *Reviews in Advance*. https://dornsife.usc.edu/wendy-wood/wp-content/uploads/sites/183/2023/10/wood.runger.2016.pdf
- Yildiz, M. (2025, March 24). How to outsmart your future self: Understanding the use of Ulysses contracts. *Medium*. https://medium.com/readers-digests/how-to-outsmart-your-future-self-understanding-the-use-of-ulysses-contracts-cf65b5c7c807
- Zapier. (2024, July 10). The 5 best habit tracker apps. *Zapier Blog*. https://zapier.com/blog/best-habit-tracker-app/
- ZCal. (2025, March 2). Buffer time: The scheduling hack to boost productivity. *ZCal Blog*. https://zcal.co/blog/buffer-time

ABOUT THE AUTHOR

Bobby L. Butler brings over four decades of hard-won experience in sales, business ownership, and human development to his mission of helping others overcome procrastination and build unstoppable productivity.

Throughout his 43-year career, Bobby and the teams he's led have generated more than $600 million in revenue across seven industries, including e-commerce, fintech, automotive, learning and development, and telecommunications. His journey spans 25 years in corporate roles, from sales representative to global accounts manager to senior sales management positions, and 18 years as a successful small business owner.

What makes Bobby's story particularly compelling is that he achieved this remarkable success as an introvert in professions that demand constant human engagement. This personal challenge with connecting to others, combined with the high-pressure demands of his roles, gave him firsthand experience with procrastination—not as a character flaw, but as a natural human response to stress, uncertainty, and over-whelming demands.

A lifelong learner, Bobby holds four college degrees and has completed extensive professional training through organizations such as the American Management Association, FranklinCovey, Xerox Corporation, and the American Society for Training and Development. He has developed and co-developed 29 training programs in sales, management, leadership, and customer service. He is the author of two previous sales books: *The Sales Producer* (1989) and *The Sales Mentor: Professional Sales 101 & 102 For The Development Years* (2003).

In recent years, Bobby has leveraged technology as a force multiplier for his mission, developing a working knowledge of artificial intelligence, automation, and programming to enhance his research, writing, and publishing capabilities and to reach a broader audience of people who need practical solutions for productivity challenges.

A U.S. Air Force veteran who served as an Air Traffic Controller and trainer from 1974 to 1978, Bobby's military service instilled in him principles of integrity, service, and excellence that have guided him throughout his personal and professional life—values that drive his commitment today to giving back through his writing.

The Procrastination Solution represents the first book in Bobby's planned self-help series, where he combines decades of real-world experience with practical, science-backed strategies that work for busy professionals, overwhelmed parents, and anyone tired of feeling behind. His mission is simple: to help others discover that procrastination isn't a character flaw—it's just a pattern that can be changed, one small step at a time.

Bobby is the proud father of two successful daughters and grandfather to a brilliant college student who shares his birthday. He lives in Tennessee, where he continues to write and develop resources to help people build more productive and fulfilling lives.